Fodor's POCKET 4th edition

prague

Excerpted from *Fodor's Eastern and Central Europe*

fodor's travel publications
new york • toronto • london • sydney • auckland
www.fodors.com

contents

maps

ON THE ROAD WITH FODOR'S

EVERY TRIP IS A SIGNIFICANT TRIP. Acutely aware of that fact, we've pulled out all stops in preparing *Fodor's Pocket Prague*. To guide you in putting together your experience, we've created multiday itineraries and city tours. And to direct you to the places that are truly worth your time and money, we've found an endearingly picky know-it-all we're pleased to call our writer. Having seen all corners of Prague, he's a real expert. If you knew him, you'd poll him for tips yourself.

Our writer, Minnesota-born **Ky Krauthamer,** came to Prague in 1992 and settled in as a journalist and freelance writer specializing in travel and culture. He has contributed to several Fodor's guides, including three editions of *Fodor's Eastern and Central Europe.*

Don't Forget to Write

Keeping a travel guide fresh and up-to-date is a big job. So we love your feedback—positive and negative—and follow up on all suggestions. Contact the *Pocket Prague* editor at editors@fodors.com or c/o Fodor's, 280 Park Avenue, New York, NY 10017. And have a wonderful trip!

Karen Cure

Editorial Director

Your checklist for a perfect journey

WAY AHEAD
· Devise a trip budget.

· Write down the five things you want most from this trip. Keep this list handy before and during your trip.

· Make plane or train reservations. Book lodging and rental cars.

· Arrange for pet care.

· Check your passport. Apply for a new one if necessary.

· Photocopy important documents and store in a safe place.

A MONTH BEFORE
· Make restaurant reservations and buy theater and concert tickets. Visit fodors.com for links to local events.

· Familiarize yourself with the local language or lingo.

TWO WEEKS BEFORE
· Replenish your supply of medications.

· Create your itinerary.

· Enjoy a book or movie set in your destination to get you in the mood.

· Develop a packing list. Shop for missing essentials. Repair and launder or dry-clean your clothes.

A WEEK BEFORE
· Stop newspaper deliveries. Pay bills.

· Acquire traveler's checks.

· Stock up on film.

· Label your luggage.

· Finalize your packing list— take less than you think you need.

· Create a toiletries kit filled with travel-size essentials.

· Get lots of sleep. Don't get sick before your trip.

A DAY BEFORE
· Drink plenty of water.

· Check your travel documents.

· Get packing!

DURING YOUR TRIP
· Keep a journal/scrapbook.

· Spend time with locals.

· Take time to explore. Don't plan too much.

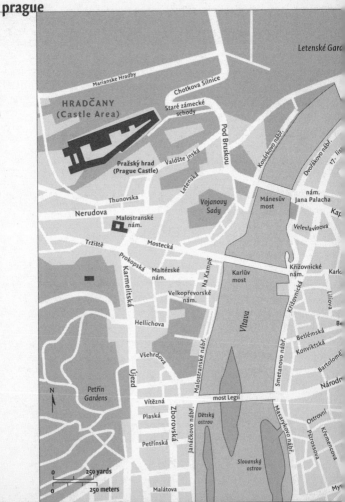

Letenské Gard

Marianske Hradby

Chotkova Silnice

HRADČANY
(Castle Area)

Staré zámecké schody

Pod Bruskou

Kosířkovo nábř.

Dvořákovo nábř.

17. lis

Pražský hrad
(Prague Castle)

Valdště jnská

Letenská

Thunovska

Vojanovy Sady

Mánesův most

nám. Jana Palacha

Kap

Nerudova

Malostranské nám.

Veleslavínova

Tržiště

Mostecká

Prokopská

Na Kampě

Karlův most

Křižovnické nám.

Karlo

Karmelitská

Maltézské nám.

Betlémská

Liliova

Be

Velkopřevorské nám.

Hellichova

Vltava

Konviktská

Bartolomě

Smetanovo nábř.

Všehrdova

Malostranské nábř.

Křižovnická

Národní

Újezd

N

Petřín Gardens

Vítězná

most Legií

Masarykovo nábř.

Ostrovní

Plaská

Zborovská

Dětský ostrov

Pštrossova

Křemencova

Petřínská

Janáčkovo nábř.

0   250 yards

0   250 meters

Malátova

Slovanský ostrov

Mys

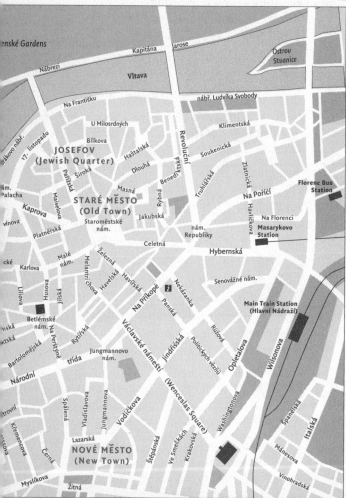

enské Gardens

Kapitána Jarose

Ostrov
Stvanice

Nábrezi

Vltava

Na Františku

nábř. Ludvíka Svobody

U Milosrdných

Klimentská

17. listopadu

Bílkova

krakovo nábr.

JOSEFOV
(Jewish Quarter)

Haštalská

Soukenická

Pařížská

Revoluční

Zlatnická

Široká

Dlouhá

Benediktská

Truhlářská

Florenc Bus
Station

nám.
Palacha

Masná

Rybná

Na Poříčí

STARÉ MĚSTO
(Old Town)

Kaprova

Maiselova

Staroměstské
nám.

Jakubská

Havlíčkova

Na Florenci

Masarykovo
Station

vinova

Platnéřská

nám.
Republiky

Celetná

Hybernská

cké

Malé
nám.

Karlova

Železná

Melantrichova

Havelská

Havlířská

Nekázanka

Senovážné nám.

Liliova

Husova

Pštrossova

Na Příkopě

Panská

Main Train Station
(Hlavní Nádraží)

Betlémské
nám.

Na Perštýně

Rytířská

Jindřišská

Politických vězňů

Růžova

Opletalova

Wilsonova

nská

Bartolomějská

třída

Jungmannovo
nám.

Václavské náměstí

Washingtonova

rktská

Národní

Vladislavova

Jungmannova

Vodičkova

(Wenceslas Square)

Španělská

Italská

trovní

Spálená

Štěpánská

Ve Smečkách

Krakovská

Mánesova

Kremencova

Černá

Lazarská

NOVÉ MĚSTO
(New Town)

sova

Myslíkova

Žitná

Vinohradská

česká republika (czech republic)

GERMANY

Görlitz

Dresden

Liberec

Chemnitz

Děčín

Jablonec

Teplice · Usti

Česká Lípa

Most

Litoměřice

Chomutov

Louny

Mladá
Boleslav

Františkovy
Lázně

Karlovy
Vary

Kolín

Cheb

Kladno

Prague

Mariánské Lázně

Beroun

Kutná
Hora

Plzeň

BOHEMIA

Příbram

Vlašim

N

Milevsko

Tábor

Jihlava

Klatovy

Písek

Strakonice

Telč

Třeboň

Český
Krumlov

České
Budějovice

Zn

GERMANY

AUSTRIA

POLAND

Wroclaw

Opole

rec
blonec

Náchod
Hradec Králové

v

lín

Pardubice
E442
Chrudim

Opava
Karviná
Ostrava
Český Těšín

Svitavy

MORAVIA

Frýdek-
Místek

Havlíčkův
Brod

Olomouc
E462
Nový Jičín

ava

Prostějov
Přerov
Vsetín

Čadca

Brno E462
Otrokovice
Zlín

Žilina

Telč

Uherské Hradiště

Martin

Dubnica

SLOVAKIA

Znojmo
Mikulov
Břeclav

D2

Trenčín
Prievidza

Nové Mesto

E75

Piešťany

Zvolen

RIA

Trnava

Nitra
Levice

Vienna

Bratislava

Dunaj
Streda

Nové
Zámky

HUNGARY

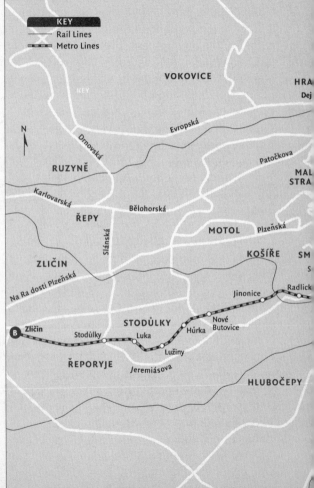

KEY
— Rail Lines
▪▪▪ Metro Lines

VOKOVICE

HRA
Dej

Evropská

Drnovská

Patočkova

MAL
STRA

N

RUZYNĚ

Karlovarská

Bělohorská

ŘEPY

MOTOL   Plzeňská

Slánská

KOŠÍŘE   SM
S

ZLIČIN

Na Ra dosti Plzeňská   Radlick

Jinonice

STODŮLKY   Nové
Butovice

Zličin   Stodůlky   Luka   Hůrka

ŘEPORYJE   Lužiny

Jeremiásova

HLUBOČEPY

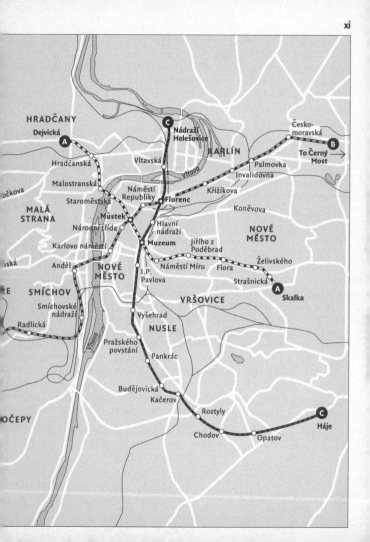

HRADČANY

Dejvická Ⓐ

Hradčanská

Malostranská

Staroměstská

Náměstí
Republiky

MALÁ
STRANA

Můstek

Národní třída

Karlovo náměstí

Anděl

NOVÉ
MĚSTO

SMÍCHOV

Smíchovské
nádraží

Radlická

Ⓒ Nádraží
Holešovice

Vltavská

KARLÍN

Palmovka

Invalidovna

Křižíkova

Ⓒ Florenc

Hlavní
nádraží

Muzeum

Jiřího z
Poděbrad

Náměstí Míru   Flora

Koněvova

Česko-
moravská

To Černý
Ⓑ Most →

NOVÉ
MĚSTO

Želivského

I.P.
Pavlova

Strašnická

Ⓐ Skalka

VRŠOVICE

Vyšehrad

NUSLE

Pražského
povstání

Pankrác

Budějovická

Kačerov

Roztyly

Chodov   Opatov

Ⓒ Háje

OČEPY

prague

In This Chapter

Updated by Ky Krauthamer and Martha Lagace

introducing prague

THE DRAMATIC PACE of change in Prague since the fall of Communism gives the city a sense of action and possibility often missing in Western capitals, breathing contemporary life into the centuries-old streets. It is here, just steps off the beaten tourist paths, where the hidden spirits that seem to govern Prague reveal themselves, transcending and even laughing at the political and social shifts of the moment.

Prague's spirit is clever and romantic, with a decidedly dark sense of humor. The easily walkable Malá Strana (Lesser Quarter), Staré Město (Old Town), and Nové Město (New Town) are all haunted alleyways and curves, some leading to hidden 13th-century churches, some coming to abrupt stops, others emptying into exuberant squares or regal gardens. Gaiety and paranoia forge an uneasy truce. Czechs themselves may scoff at you, or may invite you to their countryside cottage for a week of picking mushrooms.

This duality is packed in everywhere. Just off Wenceslas Square you can find the world's most frivolous Cubist lamp standing next to the solemn Gothic heights of the 14th-century Church of Our Lady of the Snows—and to complete the absurd picture, there's a Japanese bonsai garden in the church's backyard. St. Vitus Cathedral is a testament to architectural potlock, with one of its dark 13th-century spires topped by an 18th-century onion dome, while Gothic gargoyles sneer above Art Nouveau stained glass.

Because the city has miraculously avoided war damage over the centuries, the streets themselves are a vivid history lesson. Walk through the sad but re-emergent Jewish Quarter, where Hitler planned on "preserving" this neighborhood as a monument to the "decadent" Jewish culture he was busy annihilating. See the terrific statue of Protestant revolutionary Jan Hus on Old Town Square, where his followers were executed in that very space for insisting that the laity be allowed to take Communion with the same wine reserved for the priests, and then visit any Hussite cathedral and notice the symbolic wine goblet carved above the front door.

Visits to the National Gallery, the stunningly restored Art Nouveau Municipal House, and the cavernous Museum of Modern Art will tell you much of what you need to know about Czech history and art. You can get a feel for Prague's artistic magnetism—past and present—by catching a film, a reading, or a live band. But for true immersion, nothing beats stepping into one of a thousand neighborhood pubs, drinking the best beer in the world for 50 cents a pint, and watching as the locals spring to life when someone breaks out a guitar.

The Czech Republic is quickly distancing itself from its Communist past; soon it will have its own star on the European Union flag, and the best Czech beers will be sold for prices depressingly familiar to travelers from the West. Before the window closes, though, Prague will continue to seduce, infuriate, and even ensnare those daring enough to visit.

NEW AND NOTEWORTHY

Prague remains the hub of tourism and cultural life in the Czech Republic. As ever, the city is a dream for classical-music lovers and opera fans. The annual Prague spring music festival, which even before the collapse of the Communist government was one of the great events on the European calendar, is attracting record numbers of music lovers. Meanwhile, the Karlovy Vary International Film Festival grows ever more popular with the public—many of whom sleep on park benches during festival week every July.

The number of **hotels and restaurants** keeps pace with the growing number of visitors in Prague, now firmly established among Europe's leading tourist destinations. The arrival of visitors and long-term residents from all over the world has brought forth new restaurants offering Cajun, Indian, vegetarian, and other exotic fare alongside the traditional ones serving pork and dumplings.

Although visitor-swamped Prague hardly needed any more publicity, its role as one of nine European Cities of Culture in 2000 encouraged modest extra funding for the arts from public and private donors. A new **museum of Central European modern art** was set to open on Kampa Island by year's end.

Meanwhile, the country's industrial reform continues to gain momentum, and the Czech Republic is on track to join the European Union. The Czech Republic, along with Hungary and Poland, became NATO member states in 1999, thus accomplishing a major goal for all three nations, but at the price of alienating Russia, their former "socialist brother." President Václav Havel ends his final term in 2003, and as yet there is no clear successor in sight.

PLEASURES AND PASTIMES

DINING

Although the quality of restaurant cuisine and service in the Czech Republic remains uneven, Prague is the exception. Here, dozens of restaurants compete for an increasingly discriminating clientele. The traditional dishes—roast pork or duck with dumplings, or broiled meat with sauce—can be light and tasty when well prepared. Grilled pond trout appears on most menus and is often the tastiest item available. An annoying "cover charge" (20 Kč–50 Kč in expensive places) usually makes its way onto restaurant bills, seemingly to subsidize the salt and pepper shakers. You should discreetly check the bill, since a few unscrupulous proprietors still overcharge foreigners.

Restaurants generally fall into three categories. A *pivnice* or *hospoda* (beer hall) usually offers a simple, inexpensive menu of goulash or pork with dumplings. The atmosphere tends to be friendly and casual, and you can expect to share a table. More attractive, and more expensive, are the *vinárna* (wine cellar) and the *restaurace* (restaurant), which serve a full range of dishes. Wine cellars, some occupying Romanesque basements, can be a real treat.

Ignoring the familiar fast-food outlets that are now a common sight, the quickest and cheapest dining option is the *lahůdky* (snack bar or deli). In larger towns, the *kavárna* (café) and *čajovna* (tea house) are ever more popular—and welcome—additions to the dining scene.

Lunch, usually eaten between noon and 2, is the main meal for Czechs and the best deal. Many restaurants put out a special luncheon menu (*denní lístek*), with more appetizing selections at better prices. If you don't see it, ask your waiter. Dinner is usually served from 5 until 9 or 10, but don't wait too long to eat. Most Czechs eat only a light meal in the evening. Also, restaurant cooks frequently knock off early on slow nights, and the later you arrive, the more likely it is that the kitchen will be closed. In general, dinner menus do not differ substantially from lunch offerings, except the prices are higher.

LODGING

The Czech Republic's official hotel classification now follows the international star system. These ratings correspond closely to our categories as follows: deluxe or five-star plus four-star ($$$$); three-star ($$$); two-star ($$). The $ category will most often be met by private rooms. Often you can book rooms—

both at hotels and in private homes—through Čedok (☞ Visitor Information in Practical Information). Otherwise, try calling or writing the hotel directly. Keep in mind that in many hotels, except at the deluxe level, a "double" bed means two singles that can be pushed together. (Single-mattress double beds are generally not available.)

The prices quoted are for double rooms during high season; generally, breakfast is included in the room rate. At certain periods, such as Easter and during festivals, prices can jump 15%–25%; as a rule, always ask the price before taking a room.

SHOPPING

In Prague, Karlovy Vary, and elsewhere in Bohemia, look for elegant and unusual crystal and porcelain. Bohemia is also renowned for the quality and deep red color of its garnets; keep an eye out for beautiful garnet rings and brooches. You can also find excellent ceramics, especially in Moravia, as well as other folk artifacts, such as printed textiles, lace, hand-knit sweaters, and painted eggs. There are attractive crafts stores throughout the Czech Republic. Karlovy Vary is blessed with a variety of unique items to buy, including the strange pipelike drinking mugs used in the spas; vases left to petrify in the mineral-laden water; and *Becherovka*, a tasty herbal aperitif that makes a nice gift to take home.

WINE AND BEER

Czechs are reputed to drink more beer per capita than any people on earth; small wonder, as many connoisseurs rank Bohemian lager-style beer as the best in the world. This cool, crisp brew was invented in Plzenš (Pilsen) in 1842, although Czech beer had already been brewed for centuries prior to that time. Aside from the world-famous *Plzenšký Prazdroj* (Pilsner Urquell) and milder *Budvar* (the original Budweiser) brands, some typical beers are the slightly bitter *Krušovice*, fruity

Radegast, and the sweeter, Prague-brewed *Staropramen. Světlé pivo*, or golden beer, is most common, although many pubs also serve *černé* (dark), which is often slightly sweeter than the light variety.

Czechs also produce quite drinkable wines: peppy, fruity whites and mild, versatile reds. Southern Moravia, with comparatively warm summers and rich soil, grows the bulk of the wine harvest; look for the Mikulov and Znojmo regional designations. Favorite white varietals are *Müller Thurgau*, with a fine muscat bouquet and light flavor, and *Neuburské*, yellow-green in color and with a dry, smoky bouquet. *Rulandské bílé*, a semidry Burgundy-like white, has a flowery bouquet and full-bodied flavor. Belying the notion that northerly climes are more auspicious for white than red grapes, northern Bohemia's scant few hundred acres of vineyards produce reliable reds and the occasional jewel. *Frankovka* is fiery red and slightly acidic, while the cherry-red *Rulandské červené* is an excellent, drier choice. *Vavřinecké* is dark and slightly sweet.

QUICK TOURS

If you're here for just a short period you need to plan carefully so as to make the most of your time in Prague. The city is beautiful year-round, but in summer and during the Christmas and Easter holidays it is overrun with tourists. Spring and fall generally combine good weather with a more bearable level of tourism. In winter you'll encounter fewer visitors and have the opportunity to see Prague breathtakingly covered in snow, but it can get very cold.

The following itineraries outline major sights throughout the city, and will help you structure your visit efficiently. Each is intended to take about four hours—a perfect way to fill a free morning or afternoon. For more information about individual sights, *see* Here and There.

HRADČANY (CASTLE AREA)

Even on a short trip to Prague, you can get a strong taste of the city's historical richness and buzzing energy. Start with the hilltop **Pražský hrad** (Prague Castle), visit the soaring, Gothic **Chrám svatého Víta** (St. Vitus Cathedral) and the **Královský palác** (Royal Palace) and drink in views of the city. If you have some more time, you may want to stop into the **Strahovský klášter** (Strahov Monastery) and **Národní galerie** (National Gallery). To get to or from the castle, walk along Nerudova ulice, a steep street lined with burgher's homes; there are little restaurants if you need a break.

JOSEFOV (JEWISH GHETTO)

Head to the Josefov early in the morning before the crowds of tourists pack its tiny streets. You can also dip into the **Malá Strana** (Lesser Quarter) to see the voluptuous Baroque curves of **Chrám svatého Mikuláše** (St. Nicholas Church). If you're interested in modern architecture, head to the **Nové Město** (New Town), where you can see the "Fred and Ginger" building by Frank Gehry and Vlado Milunić as well as several Cubist buildings.

STARÉ MĚSTO (OLD TOWN)

Try to time your visit to the stunning **Starom stské náměstí** (Old Town Square) to coincide with the hourly performance of the astronomical clock on the **Starom stská radnice** (Old Town Hall); you can also visit the Gothic-on-the-outside, Baroque-on-the-inside **Kostel Panny Marie před Týnem** (Týn Church).

VÁCLAVSKÉ NÁMĚSTÍ (WENCESLAS SQUARE)

Stretching southeast of the Old Town is **Václavské náměstí**, actually a long avenue humming with activity—be sure to duck into some of the arcades that branch off the boulevard. In the evening, go back towards the river for the unforgettable view from the statue-lined **Karlův most** (Charles Bridge).

In This Chapter

Updated by Ky Krauthamer

here and there

IN THE YEARS SINCE NOVEMBER 17, 1989, when Prague's students took to the streets to help bring down the 40-year-old Communist regime, the city has enjoyed an exhilarating cultural renaissance. Amid Prague's cobblestone streets and gold-tip spires, new galleries, cafés, and clubs teem with young Czechs (the middle-aged are generally too busy trying to make a living) and members of the city's colony of "expatriates." New shops and, perhaps most noticeably, scads of new restaurants have opened, expanding the city's culinary reach far beyond the traditional roast pork and dumplings. Many have something to learn in the way of presentation and service, but Praguers still marvel at a variety that was unthinkable not so many years ago.

The arts and theater are also thriving in the "new" Prague. Young playwrights, some writing in English, regularly stage their own works. Weekly poetry readings are standing room only. Classical music maintains its famous standards, while rock, jazz, and dance clubs are jammed nightly. The arts of the new era—nonverbal theater, "installation" art, world music— are as trendy in Prague as in any European capital, but possess a distinctive Czech flavor.

All of this frenetic activity plays well against a stunning backdrop of towering churches and centuries-old bridges and alleyways. Prague achieved much of its present glory in the 14th century, during the long reign of Charles IV, king of Bohemia and Moravia and Holy Roman Emperor. It was Charles who established a university in the city and laid out the New Town, charting Prague's growth.

During the 15th century, the city's development was hampered by the Hussite Wars, a series of crusades launched by the Holy Roman Empire to subdue the fiercely independent Czech noblemen. The Czechs were eventually defeated in 1620 at the Battle of White Mountain (Bílá Hora) near Prague and were ruled by the Hapsburg family for the next 300 years. Under the Hapsburgs, Prague became a German-speaking city and an important administrative center, but it was forced to play second fiddle to the monarchy's capital, Vienna. Much of the Lesser Quarter, on the left bank of the Vltava, was built up at this time, becoming home to Austrian nobility and its Baroque tastes.

Prague regained its status as a national capital in 1918, with the creation of the modern Czechoslovak state, and quickly asserted itself in the interwar period as a vital cultural center. Although the city escaped World War II essentially intact, Czechoslovakia fell under the political and cultural domination of the Soviet Union until the 1989 popular uprisings. The election of dissident playwright Václav Havel to the post of national president set the stage for the city's renaissance, which has since proceeded at a dizzying, quite Bohemian rate.

Numbers in the text correspond to numbers in the margin and on the Prague map.

STARÉ MĚSTO (OLD TOWN)
A Good Walk

Ever-hopping Wenceslas Square (☞ Nové Město [New Town] and Vyšehrad, *below*), convenient to hotels and transportation, is an excellent place to begin a tour of the Old Town, although it actually lies within the New Town. To begin the approach to the Old Town proper, start at the lower end of the square, walk past the tall, Art Deco Koruna complex, and turn right onto the handsome pedestrian zone of **Na Příkopě**. Turn left onto Havířská ulice and follow this small alley to the glittering green-and-cream splendor of the 18th-century theater called the **Stavovské divadlo** ①.

Return to Na Příkopě, turn left, and continue to the end of the street. On weekdays between 8 AM and 5 PM, it's well worth taking a peek at the stunning interior of the Živnostenská banka (Merchant's Bank), at No. 20.

Na Příkopě ends abruptly at náměstí Republiky (Republic Square), an important New Town transportation hub (with a metro stop). The severe depression-era facade of the Česká Národní banka (at Na Příkopě 30) makes the building look more like a fortress than the nation's central bank. Close by stands a stately tower, the **Prašná brána**, its festive Gothic spires looming above the square. Adjacent to this dignified building, the **Obecní dům** ② concert hall looks decidedly decadent.

Walk through the arch at the base of the Prašná brána and down the formal **Celetná ulice** ③, the first leg of the so-called Royal Way. Monarchs favored this route primarily because the houses along Celetná were among the city's finest, providing a suitable backdrop to the coronation procession. The pink U Sixtu (Sixt House), at Celetná 2, sports one of the street's handsomest, if restrained, Baroque facades. Baroque influence is even visible in the Cubist department store **Dům U černé Matky Boží** ④, now a museum.

Staroměstské náměstí ⑤, at the end of Celetná, is dazzling, thanks partly to the double-spired **Kostel Panny Marie před Týnem** ⑥, which rises over the square from behind a row of patrician houses. To the immediate left of this church, at No. 13, is Dům U Kamenného zvonu (House at the Stone Bell), a Baroque town house that has been stripped down to its original Gothic elements.

Next door stands the gorgeous pink-and-ocher **Palác Kinských**. At this end of the square, you can't help noticing the expressive **Jan Hus monument** ⑦. Just beyond is the Gothic **Staroměstská radnice** ⑧, which, with its impressive 200-ft tower, gives the square its sense of importance. As the hour approaches, join the crowds milling below the tower's 15th-century astronomical clock for a brief but spooky spectacle taken straight from the Middle Ages, every hour on the hour.

The square's second church, the Baroque **Kostel svatého Mikuláše** ⑨, is not to be confused with the Lesser Quarter's Chrám svatého Mikuláše on the other side of the river (☞ Karlùv most [Charles Bridge] and Malá Strana [Lesser Quarter], *below*). For a small detour, head down Kaprova street to the **Rudolfinum** ⑩ concert hall and gallery; across the street is the Uměleckoprùmyslové muzeum (Museum of Decorative Arts). Both are notable neo-Renaissance buildings.

Returning to Staroměstské náměstí, you'll find the **Franz Kafka Exposition** adjoining Kostel svatého Mikuláše on náměstí Franze Kafky, a little square that used to be part of U Radnice street. Continue along U Radnice proper just a few yards until you come to **Malé náměstí** ⑪, a minisquare with arcades on one side. Look for tiny Karlova ulice, which begins in the southwest corner of the square, and take another quick right to stay on it (watch the signs—this medieval street seems designed to confound the visitor). At the České muzeum výtvarných umění (Czech Museum of Fine Arts), pause and inspect the exotic **Clam-Gallas palác** ⑫, behind you at Husova 20. You'll recognize it easily: look for the Titans in the doorway holding up what must be a very heavy Baroque facade. Head the other way down Husova for a glimpse of ecstatic Baroque stuffed inside somber Gothic at the **Kostel svatého Jiljí** ⑬, at No. 8.

Continue walking along Husova to Na Perštýně and turn right at tiny Betlémská ulice. The alley opens up onto a quiet square,

Betlémské náměstí, and upon the most revered of all Hussite churches in Prague, the **Betlémská kaple** ⑭.

Return to Na Perštýně and continue walking to the right. As you near the back of the buildings of the busy Národní třída (National Boulevard), turn left at Martinská ulice. At the end of the street, the forlorn but majestic church **Kostel svatého Martina ve zdi** ⑮ stands like a postwar ruin. Walk around the church to the left and through a little archway of apartments onto the bustling Národní třída. To the left, a five-minute walk away, lies Wenceslas Square and the starting point of the walk.

TIMING

Wenceslas Square and Old Town Square are busy with activity around-the-clock almost all year-round. If you're in search of a little peace and quiet, you will find the streets at their most subdued on early weekend mornings or right after a sudden downpour. The streets in this walking tour are reasonably close together and can be covered in half a day. Remember to be in the Old Town Square just before the hour if you want to see the astronomical clock in action.

Sights to See

⑭ **BETLÉMSKÁ KAPLE** (Bethlehem Chapel). The church's elegant simplicity is in stark contrast to the diverting Gothic and Baroque of the rest of the city. The original structure dates from the end of the 14th century, and the Czech religious reformer Jan Hus was a regular preacher here from 1402 until his exile in 1412. After the Thirty Years' War the church fell into the hands of the Jesuits and was finally demolished in 1786. Excavations carried out after World War I uncovered the original portal and three windows, and the entire church was reconstructed during the 1950s. Although little remains of the first church, some remnants of Hus's teachings can still be read on the inside walls. *Betlémské nám. 5. 30 Kč. Daily 10–5.*

exploring prague

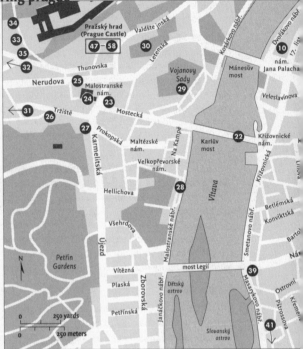

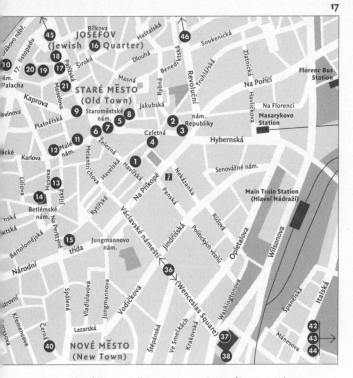

Obecní dům, 2
Pavilon, 44
Pinkasova
synagóga, 19
Rudolfinum, 10
Schönbornský
palác, 26
Schwarzen-
berský
palác, 35

Španělská
synagóga, 16
Staroměstská
radnice, 8
Staroměstské
náměstí, 5
Staronová
synagóga, 18
Starý židovský
hřbitov, 20

Statue of St.
Wenceslas, 37
Stavovské
divadlo, 1
Strahovský
klášter, 31
Václavské
náměstí, 36
Veletržní
palác, 46

Vojanovy
sady, 29
Vrtbovská
zahrada, 27
Vyšehrad, 41
Zahrada
Valdštejnského
paláce, 30
Židovská
radnice, 17

❸ CELETNÁ ULICE. Most of this street's facades indicate the buildings are from the 17th or 18th century, but appearances are deceiving: many of the houses in fact have foundations dating from the 12th century. **U Sixtu** (Sixt House), at Celetná 2, dates from the 12th century—its Romanesque vaults are still visible in the cellar. The house is being converted into a luxury hotel, due to open in 2001.

⓬ CLAM-GALLAS PALÁC (Clam-Gallas Palace). The beige-and-brown palace dates from 1713–29 and is the work of Johann Bernhard Fischer von Erlach, the famed Viennese architectural virtuoso of the day. Enter the building for a glimpse of the finely carved staircase, the work of the master himself, and of the Italian frescoes featuring Apollo that surround it. The building now houses the municipal archives and is rarely open to visitors (so walk in as if you have business there). *Husova 20.*

❹ DÙM U ČERNÉ MATKY BOŽÍ (House of the Black Madonna). In the second decade of the 20th century, young Czech architects boldly applied Cubism's radical reworking of visual space to structures. Adding a decided jolt to the architectural styles along Celetná, this Cubist building, designed by Josef Gočár, is unflinchingly modern yet topped with an almost Baroque tile roof. It now houses a permanent exhibit of Czech Cubist design and hosts temporary art shows. *Celetná 34, tel. 02/2421–1732. 35 Kč. Tues.–Sun. 10–6.*

FRANZ KAFKA EXPOSITION. Kafka was born on July 3, 1883, in a house next to the Kostel svatého Mikuláše (Church of St. Nicholas). For years the writer was only grudgingly acknowledged by the Communist cultural bureaucrats, reflecting the traditionally ambiguous attitude of the Czech government toward his work. The Communists were always too uncomfortable with Kafka's themes of bureaucracy and alienation to sing his praises loudly, if at all. As a German and a Jew, moreover, Kafka could easily be dismissed as standing outside the mainstream of Czech literature. Following the 1989 revolution, however, Kafka's popularity soared, and his works are now widely available in Czech. Only the portal of the original house remains; inside the building is a fascinating little exhibit (mostly photographs) on Kafka's life, with commentary in English. *Nám. Franze Kafky 3 (formerly U Radnice 5). 50 Kč. Tues.–Fri. 10–6, Sat. 10–5.*

❼ JAN HUS MONUMENT. Few memorials have elicited as much controversy as this one, which was dedicated in July 1915, exactly 500 years after Hus was burned at the stake in Constance, Germany. Some maintain that the monument's Secessionist style (the inscription seems to come right from turn-of-the-20th-century Vienna) clashes with the Gothic and Baroque of the square. Others dispute the romantic depiction of Hus, who appears here in flowing garb as tall and bearded. The real Hus, historians maintain, was short and had a baby face. Still, no one can take issue with the influence of this fiery preacher, whose ability to transform doctrinal disputes, both literally and metaphorically, into the language of the common man made him a religious and national symbol for the Czechs. *Staroměstské nám.*

KLÁŠTER SVATÉ ANEŽKY ČESKÉ (St. Agnes's Convent). Situated near the river between Pařížská and Revoluční streets, this peaceful complex has Prague's first buildings in the Gothic style, built from the 1230s to the 1280s. The convent is to be home to the National Gallery's marvelous collection of Czech Gothic art, which was scheduled to be moved here from the Klášter svatého Jiří in Prague Castle (☞ *below*) at the end of 2000. Check the status of this maneuver at a visitor bureau or any gallery branch. *U Milosrdných 17, tel. 02/2481–0628. 90 Kč. Tues.–Sun. 10–6.*

★ ❻ KOSTEL PANNY MARIE PŘED TÝNEM (Church of the Virgin Mary Before Týn). The exterior of the church is one of the best examples of Prague Gothic and is in part the work of Peter Parler, architect of the Charles Bridge and Chrám svatého Víta (St. Vitus's

Cathedral). Construction of its twin black-spire towers was begun later, by King Jiří of Poděbrad in 1461, during the heyday of the Hussites. Jiří had a gilded chalice, the symbol of the Hussites, proudly displayed on the front gable between the two towers. Following the defeat of the Czech Protestants by the Catholic Hapsburgs, the chalice was removed and eventually replaced by a Madonna. As a final blow, the chalice was melted down and made into the Madonna's glimmering halo (you can still see it by walking into the center of the square and looking up between the spires). The entrance to the church is through the arcades on Old Town Square, under the house at No. 604.

Much of the interior, including the tall nave, was rebuilt in the Baroque style in the 17th century. Some Gothic pieces remain, however: look to the left of the main altar for a beautifully preserved set of early Gothic carvings. The main altar itself was painted by Karel Škréta, a luminary of the Czech Baroque. Before leaving the church, look for the grave marker (tucked away to the right of the main altar) of the great Danish astronomer Tycho Brahe, who came to Prague as "Imperial Mathematicus" in 1599 under Rudolf II. As a scientist, Tycho had a place in history that is assured: Johannes Kepler (another resident of the Prague court) used Tycho's observations to formulate his laws of planetary motion. But it is myth that has endeared Tycho to the hearts of Prague residents. The robust Dane, who was apparently fond of duels, lost part of his nose in one (take a closer look at the marker). He quickly had a wax nose fashioned for everyday use but preferred to parade around on holidays and festive occasions sporting a bright silver one. *Staroměstské nám., between Celetná and Týnská. Hrs vary.*

⑬ **KOSTEL SVATÉHO JILJÍ** (Church of St. Giles). This was another important outpost of Czech Protestantism in the 16th century. The exterior is a powerful example of Gothic architecture, including the buttresses and a characteristic portal. The interior, as in many important Czech churches, is Baroque, with a design by Johann

Bernhard Fischer von Erlach and sweeping frescoes by Václav Reiner. The interior can be viewed during the day from the vestibule or at the evening concerts held several times a week. *Husova 8.*

⑮ **KOSTEL SVATÉHO MARTINA VE ZDI** (Church of St. Martin-in-the-Wall). It was here in 1414 that Holy Communion was first given to the Bohemian laity in the form of both bread and wine, in defiance of the Catholic custom of the time, which dictated that only bread was to be offered to the masses, with wine reserved for the priests and clergy. From then on, the chalice came to symbolize the Hussite movement. The church is open for evening concerts held several times each week. *Martinská ul.*

⑨ **KOSTEL SVATÉHO MIKULÁŠE** (Church of St. Nicholas). Designed in the 18th century by Prague's own master of late Baroque, Kilian Ignaz Dientzenhofer, this church is probably less successful in capturing the style's lyric exuberance than its namesake across town, the Chrám svatého Mikuláše. Still, Dientzenhofer utilized the limited space to create a well-balanced structure. The interior is compact, with a beautiful but small chandelier and an enormous black organ that seems to overwhelm the rear of the church. The church hosts almost continuous afternoon and evening tourist concerts. *Staroměstské nám. Apr.–Oct., Mon. noon–4, Tues.–Sat. 10–4, Sun. noon–3; Nov.–Mar., Tues.–Fri. and Sun. 10–noon (Wed. until 4).*

⑪ **MALÉ NÁMĚSTÍ** (Small Square). Note the iron fountain dating from around 1560 in the center of the square. The colorfully painted house at No. 3, originally a hardware store, is not as old as it looks, but here and there you will find authentic Gothic portals and Renaissance sgraffiti that betray the square's true age.

NA PŘÍKOPĚ. The name means "At the Moat" and harks back to the time when the street was indeed a moat separating the Old Town from the New Town. Today the pedestrian zone, Na Příkopěis, is prime shopping territory. At No. 19 an oversize new building, one of the worst excesses of the 1990s in Prague, houses a Marks & Spencer store. Have a look at the chic, hard-edged black-and-white Černá Růže (Black Rose) arcade at No. 12.

2 **OBECNÍ DŮM** (Municipal House). The city's Art Nouveau showpiece still fills the role it had when it was completed in 1911: it's a center for concerts, rotating art exhibits, and the café society. The mature Art Nouveau style recalls the lengths the Czech middle classes went to at the turn of the 20th century to imitate Paris, then the epitome of style and glamour. Much of the interior bears the work of Art Nouveau master Alfons Mucha, Max Švabinský, and other leading Czech artists. Mucha decorated the Hall of the Lord Mayor with impressive, magical frescoes depicting Czech history; unfortunately it's not open to the public. The beautiful **Smetanova síň** (Smetana Hall), which hosts concerts by the Prague Symphony Orchestra as well as international guests, is on the second floor. The ground-floor café is touristy, but a lovely sight with its glimmering chandeliers and exquisite woodwork. There's also a beer hall in the cellar with passable beer and mediocre food and superbly executed ceramic murals on the walls. *Nám. Republiky 5, tel. 02/2200–2100. Information center and box office daily 10–6.*

NEED A BREAK? If you prefer subtle elegance, head around the corner to the café at the **Hotel Paříž** (U Obecního domu 1, tel. 02/2422–2151), a Jugendstil jewel tucked away on a relatively quiet street.

PALÁC KINSKÝCH (Kinský Palace). This exuberant building, built in 1765 from Kilian Ignaz Dientzenhofer's design, is considered one of Prague's finest late-Baroque structures. With its exaggerated pink overlay and numerous statues, the facade looks extreme when contrasted with the more staid Baroque elements of other nearby buildings. (The interior, however, was "modernized" under Communism.) The palace once housed a German school—where Franz Kafka was a student for nine years—and presently contains the National Gallery's graphics collection. At press time exhibitions were scheduled to reopen by the end of 2000 following reconstruction of the interior. It was from this building that Communist leader Klement Gottwald, flanked by his Slovak comrade Vladimír Clementis, first addressed the crowds after seizing power in February 1948—an event recounted in the first chapter of Milan Kundera's novel *The Book of Laughter and Forgetting*. *Staroměstské nám.* 12.

PRAŠNÁ BRÁNA (Powder Tower). Construction of the tower, which replaced one of the city's 13 original gates, was begun by King Vladislav II of Jagiello in 1475. At the time, the kings of Bohemia maintained their royal residence next door, on the site of the current Obecní dùm (☞ *above*), and the tower was intended to be the grandest gate of all. But Vladislav was Polish and thus heartily disliked by the rebellious Czech citizens of Prague. Nine years after he assumed power, fearing for his life, he moved the royal court across the river to Prague Castle. Work on the tower was abandoned, and the half-finished structure was used for storing gunpowder—hence its odd name—until the end of the 17th century. The oldest part of the tower is the base. The golden spires were not added until the end of the 19th century. Climb to the top for a striking view of the Old Town and Prague Castle in the distance. *Nám. Republiky.* 20 Kč. Apr.–Oct., daily 9–6.

⑩ RUDOLFINUM. Thanks to a thorough makeover and exterior sandblasting, this neo-Renaissance monument designed by Josef Zítek and Josef Schulz presents the cleanest, brightest stonework in the city. Completed in 1884 and named for then–Hapsburg Crown Prince Rudolf, the rather low-slung sandstone building was meant to be a combination concert hall and exhibition gallery. After 1918 it was converted into the parliament of the newly independent Czechoslovakia until German invaders reinstated the concert hall in 1939. Czech writer Jiří Weil's novel *Mendelssohn Is on the Roof* tells of the cruel farce that ensued when officials ordered the removal of the Jewish composer's statue from the roof balustrade. Now the Czech Philharmonic has its home base here. The 1,200-seat **Dvořákova síň** (Dvořák Hall) has superb acoustics (the box office faces 17. listopadu). *Nám. Jana Palacha, tel. 02/2489–3111.*

Behind Dvořák Hall is a set of large exhibition rooms, the **Galerie Rudolfinum**, an innovative, state-supported gallery for rotating shows of contemporary art. Four or five large shows are mounted here annually, showcasing Czech work along with international artists, such as photographer Cindy Sherman. *Alšovo nábř. 12, tel. 02/2489–3205. 40 Kč. Tues.–Sun. 10–6.*

★ ⑧ **STAROMĚSTSKÁ RADNICE** (Old Town Hall). This is one of Prague's magnets: hundreds of people gravitate to it to see the hour struck by the mechanical figures of the **astronomical clock**. Just before the hour, look to the upper part of the clock, where a skeleton begins by tolling a death knell and turning an hourglass upside down. The Twelve Apostles parade momentarily, and then a cockerel flaps its wings and crows, piercing the air as the hour finally strikes. To the right of the skeleton, the dreaded Turk nods his head, seemingly hinting at another invasion like those of the 16th and 17th centuries. This small spectacle doesn't clue viewers in to the way this 15th-century marvel indicates the time—by the season, the zodiac sign, and the positions of the sun and moon. The calendar under the clock dates from the mid-19th century.

The Old Town Hall served as the center of administration for the Old Town beginning in 1338, when King John of Luxembourg first granted the city council the right to a permanent location. The impressive 200-ft **Town Hall Tower**, where the clock is mounted, was first built in the 14th century and given its current late-Gothic appearance around 1500 by the master Matyáš Rejsek. For a rare view of the Old Town and its maze of crooked streets and alleyways, climb the ramp or ride the elevator to the top of the tower.

If you walk around the hall to the left, you'll see it's actually a series of houses jutting into the square; they were purchased over the years and successively added to the complex. On the other side, jagged stonework reveals where a large, neo-Gothic wing once adjoined the tower until it was destroyed during fighting between townspeople and Nazi troops in May 1945.

Guided tours (most guides speak English, and English texts are on hand) of the Old Town Hall depart from the main desk inside. However, the only notable features are the fine Renaissance ceilings, the Gothic Council Room, and the Gothic chapel, where you can see the clock's apostles up close. *Staroměstské nám. Tower 30 Kč, tours 30 Kč each. Tues.–Sun. 9–6, Mon. 11–6 (until 5, Oct.–Apr.).*

★ ❺ **STAROMĚSTSKÉ NÁMĚSTÍ** (Old Town Square). There are places that, on first glimpse, stop you dead in your tracks in sheer wonder. Old Town Square is one such place. Long the heart of the Old Town, the square grew to its present proportions when the city's original marketplace was moved away from the river in the 12th century. Its shape and appearance have changed little over the years. During the day the square has a festive atmosphere as musicians vie for the favor of onlookers and artists display renditions of Prague street scenes. At night, the gaudily lit towers of the Church of the Virgin Mary before Týn rise ominously over the glowing Baroque facades. The crowds thin out, and the ghosts of the square's stormy past return.

During the 15th century the square was the focal point of conflict between Czech Hussites and German Catholics. In 1422 the radical Hussite preacher Jan Želivský was executed here for his part in storming the New Town's town hall three years earlier (☞ Karlovo náměstí in Nové Město [New Town] and Vyšehrad, *below*). In the 1419 uprising, three Catholic consuls and seven German citizens were thrown out the window—the first of Prague's many famous defenestrations. Within a few years, the

Hussites had taken over the town, expelled the Germans, and set up their own administration.

Twenty-seven white crosses set flat in the paving stones in the square, at the Old Town Hall's base, mark the spot where 27 Bohemian noblemen were killed by the Hapsburgs in 1621 during the dark days following the defeat of the Czechs at the Battle of White Mountain. The grotesque spectacle, designed to quash any further national or religious opposition, took some five hours to complete, as the men were put to the sword or hanged one by one.

One of the square's most interesting houses, at No. 3, juts out into the small extension leading into Malé náměstí. This house is called **U Minuty,** and has 16th-century Renaissance sgraffiti of biblical and classical motifs. The young Franz Kafka lived here in the 1890s.

❶ STAVOVSKÉ DIVADLO (Estates Theater). Built in the 1780s in the classical style, this handsome theater was for many years a beacon of Czech-language culture in a city long dominated by the German variety. It is probably best known as the site of the world premiere of Mozart's opera *Don Giovanni* in October 1787, with the composer himself conducting. Prague audiences were quick to acknowledge Mozart's genius: the opera was an instant hit here, though it flopped nearly everywhere else in Europe. Mozart wrote most of the opera's second act in Prague at the Villa Bertramka (☞ Karlův most [Charles Bridge] and Malá Strana [Lesser Quarter], *below*), where he was a frequent guest. *Ovocný trh 1, tel. 02/2421–5001 (box office).*

JOSEFOV (JEWISH QUARTER)

Prague's Jews survived centuries of discrimination, but two unrelated events of modern times have left their historic ghetto little more than a collection of museums. Around 1900, city officials decided for hygienic purposes to raze the minuscule neighborhood—it had ceased to be a true ghetto with the political reforms of 1848–49, and by this time the majority of its residents were poor Gentiles—and pave over its crooked streets. Only some of the synagogues, the town hall, and the cemetery survived this early attempt at urban renewal. The second event was the Holocaust. Under Nazi occupation, a staggering percentage of the city's Jews were deported or murdered in concentration camps. Of the 35,000 Jews living in Prague before World War II, only about 1,200 returned to resettle the city after the war. The community is still tiny. Only a scant few Jews, mostly elderly, live in the "ghetto" today.

Treasures and artifacts of the ghetto are now the property of the **Židovské muzeum v Praze** (Prague Jewish Museum; tel. 02/231–7191), which includes the Old Jewish Cemetery and collections installed in four surviving synagogues and the Ceremony Hall. (The Staronová synagóga, or Old-New Synagogue, a functioning house of worship, technically does not belong to the museum, but the Prague Jewish Community oversees both.) The museum was founded in 1906, but traces the vast majority of its holdings to the Nazis' destruction of 150 Jewish communities in Bohemia and Moravia. Dedicated museum workers, nearly all of whom were to die at Nazi hands, gathered and cataloged the stolen artifacts under German supervision. Exhibitions were even held during the war. A ticket good for all museum sites may be purchased at any of the synagogues but the Old-New Synagogue; single-site tickets apply only at the Old-New Synagogue and during occasional exhibits at the Spanish Synagogue. All museum sites are closed Saturday and Jewish holidays.

A Good Walk

To reach the Jewish Quarter, leave Old Town Square via handsome Pařížská ulice, centerpiece of the urban renewal effort, and head north toward the river. The festive atmosphere changes suddenly as you enter the area of the ghetto. The buildings are lower here; the mood is hushed. Take a right on

Široká and stroll two blocks down to the recently restored **Španělská synagóga** ⑯. Head back the other way, past Pařížská, turn right on Maiselova, and you'll come to the **Židovská radnice** ⑰, home to the Jewish Community Center. Adjoining it on Červená is the 16th-century High Synagogue. Across the street, at Červená 2, you see the **Staronová synagóga** ⑱, the oldest surviving synagogue in Prague.

Go west on the little street U starého hřbitova. The main museum ticket office is at the **Klausová synagóga** at No. 3A. Next door, separated from the synagogue by the exit gate of the Old Jewish Cemetery, is the former building of the Jewish Burial Society, **Obřadní síň,** which exhibits traditional Jewish funeral objects.

Return to Maiselova and follow it to Široká. Turn right to find the **Pinkasova synagóga** ⑲, a handsome Gothic structure. Also here is the entrance to the Jewish ghetto's most astonishing sight, the **Starý židovský hřbitov** ⑳.

Return to Maiselova once more and turn right in the direction of the Old Town. Look in at the displays of Czech Jewish history in the **Maiselova synagóga** ㉑.

TIMING

The Jewish Quarter is one of the most popular visitor destinations in Prague, especially in the height of summer, when its tiny streets are bursting with tourists almost all the time. The best time for a quieter visit is early morning when the museums and cemetery first open. The area itself is very compact, and a fairly thorough tour should only take half a day.

Sights to See

KLAUSOVÁ SYNAGÓGA (Klausen Synagogue). This Baroque former synagogue was built at the end of the 17th century in the place of three small buildings (a synagogue, school, and ritual bath) that were destroyed in a fire that devastated the ghetto in

1689. Inside, displays of Czech Jewish traditions emphasize celebrations and daily life. *U starého hřbitova 3A. Combined ticket to museum sites and Old-New Synagogue, 480 Kč; museum sites only, 280 Kč. Apr.–Oct., Sun.–Fri. 9–6; Nov.–Mar., Sun.–Fri. 9–4:30.*

㉑ MAISELOVA SYNAGÓGA (Maisel Synagogue). Here, the history of Czech Jews from the 10th to the 18th century is illustrated with the aid of some of the Prague Jewish Museum's most precious objects, including silver Torah shields and pointers, spice boxes, and candelabra; historic tombstones; and fine ceremonial textiles, including some donated by Mordechai Maisel to the synagogue he founded. The richest items come from the late 16th and early 17th century—a prosperous era for Prague's Jews. *Maiselova 10. Combined ticket to museum sites and Old-New Synagogue, 480 Kč; museum sites only, 280 Kč. Apr.–Oct., Sun.–Fri. 9–6; Nov.–Mar., Sun.–Fri. 9–4:30.*

OBŘADNÍ SÍŇ (Ceremony Hall). In this neo-Romanesque building, the focus is on rather grim subjects: Jewish funeral paraphernalia, old gravestones, and medical instruments. Special attention is paid to the activities of the Jewish Burial Society through many fine objects and paintings. *U starého hřbitova 3A. Combined ticket to museum sites and Old-New Synagogue, 480 Kč; museum sites only, 280 Kč. Apr.–Oct., Sun.–Fri. 9–6; Nov.–Mar., Sun.–Fri. 9–4:30.*

⑲ PINKASOVA SYNAGÓGA (Pinkas Synagogue). This synagogue has two particularly moving testimonies to the appalling crimes perpetrated against the Jews during World War II. One tribute astounds by sheer numbers: The inside walls are covered with nearly 80,000 names of Bohemian and Moravian Jews murdered by the Nazis. Among them are the names of the paternal grandparents of former U.S. Secretary of State Madeleine Albright, who learned of their fate only in 1997. There is also an exhibition of drawings made by children at the Nazi concentration camp Terezín in Northern Bohemia. The Nazis used the camp for propaganda purposes to demonstrate their "humanity" toward the Jews, and prisoners were given relative freedom to lead "normal" lives. However, transports to death camps in Poland began in earnest in 1944, and many thousands of Terezín prisoners, including many of these children, eventually perished. *Enter from Široká 3. Combined ticket to museum sites and Old-New Synagogue, 480 Kč; museum sites only, 280 Kč. Apr.–Oct., Sun.–Fri. 9–6; Nov.–Mar., Sun.–Fri. 9–4:30.*

★ ⓰ **ŠPANĚLSKÁ SYNAGÓGA** (Spanish Synagogue). A domed Moorish-style synagogue was built in 1868 on the site of the Altschul, the city's oldest synagogue. Here, the historical exposition that begins in the Maisel Synagogue (☞ *above*) continues, taking the story up to the post–World War II period. The displays are not that compelling, but the building's painstakingly restored interior definitely is. *Vězeňská 1. Combined ticket to museum sites and Old-New Synagogue, 480 Kč; museum sites only, 280 Kč. Apr.–Oct., Sun.–Fri. 9–6; Nov.–Mar., Sun.–Fri. 9–4:30.*

★ ⓲ **STARONOVÁ SYNAGÓGA** (Old-New Synagogue, or Altneuschul). Dating from the mid-13th century, this is one of the most important works of early Gothic in Prague. The odd name recalls the legend that the synagogue was built on the site of an ancient Jewish temple and that stones from the temple were used to build the present structure. The oldest part of the synagogue is the entrance, with its vault supported by two pillars. The synagogue has not only survived fires and the razing of the ghetto at the end of the last century, but also emerged from the Nazi occupation intact; it is still in active use. As the oldest synagogue in Europe that still serves its original function, it is a living storehouse of Bohemian Jewish life. Note that men are required to cover their heads inside and that during services men and women sit apart. *Červená 2. Combined ticket to Old-New Synagogue and museum sites, 480 Kč; Old-New Synagogue only, 200 Kč. Apr.–Oct., Sun.–Thurs. 9–6; Nov.–Mar., Sun.–Thurs. 9–4:30; closes 2–3 hrs early on Fri.*

★ ⓴ **STARÝ ŽIDOVSKÝ HŘBITOV** (Old Jewish Cemetery). This unforgettably melancholy sight not far from the busy city was, from the 15th century to 1787, the final resting place for all Jews living in Prague. The confined space forced graves to be piled one on top of the other. Tilted at crazy angles, the 12,000 visible tombstones are but a fraction of countless thousands more buried below. Walk the path amid the gravestones; the relief symbols you see represent the names and professions of the deceased. The oldest marked grave belongs to the poet Avigdor Kara, who died in 1439; the grave is not accessible from the pathway, but the original tombstone can be seen in the Maisel Synagogue. The best-known marker is that of Jehuda ben Bezalel, the famed Rabbi Loew (died 1609), a chief rabbi of Prague and profound scholar who is credited with creating the mythical Golem. Even today, small scraps of paper bearing wishes are stuffed into the cracks of the rabbi's tomb in the hope he will grant them. Loew's grave lies near the exit. *Široká 3. Combined ticket to museum sites and Old-New Synagogue, 480 Kč; museum sites only, 280 Kč. Apr.–Oct., Sun.–Fri. 9–6; Nov.–Mar., Sun.–Fri. 9–4:30. www.jewishmuseum.cz*

⓱ **ŽIDOVSKÁ RADNICE** (Jewish Town Hall). The hall was the creation of Mordechai Maisel, an influential Jewish leader at the end of the 16th century. It was restored in the 18th century and given its clock and bell tower at that time. A second clock, with Hebrew numbers, keeps time counterclockwise. Now home to the Jewish Community Center, the building also houses a kosher restaurant, Shalom. *Maiselova 18.*

KARLÙV MOST (CHARLES BRIDGE) AND MALÁ STRANA (LESSER QUARTER)

One of Prague's most exquisite neighborhoods, the Lesser Quarter (or Little Town) was established in 1257 and for years was home to the merchants and craftsmen who served the royal court. The Lesser Quarter is not for the methodical traveler. Its charm lies in the tiny lanes, the sudden blasts of bombastic architecture, and the soul-stirring views that emerge for a second before disappearing behind the sloping roofs.

A Good Walk

Begin your tour on the Old Town side of **Karlův most** ㉒, which you can reach by foot in about 10 minutes from the Old Town Square. Rising above it is the majestic **Staroměstská mostecká věž.** The climb of 138 steps is worth the effort for the view you'll get of the Old Town and, across the river, of the Lesser Quarter and Prague Castle.

It's worth pausing to take a closer look at some of the statues as you walk across Karlův most toward the Lesser Quarter. You'll see Kampa Island below you, separated from the mainland by an arm of the Vltava known as Čertovka (Devil's Stream).

By now you are almost at the end of the bridge. In front of you is the striking conjunction of the two Malá Strana bridge towers, one Gothic, the other Romanesque. Together they frame the Baroque flamboyance of Chrám svatého Mikuláše in the distance. At night this is an absolutely wondrous sight.

Walk under the gateway of the towers into the little, uphill street called Mostecká. You have now entered the Lesser Quarter. Follow Mostecká up to the rectangular **Malostranské náměstí** ㉓, now the district's traffic hub rather than its heart. In the middle of the square stands **Chrám svatého Mikuláše** ㉔.

Nerudova ulice ㉕ runs up from the square toward Prague Castle. Lined with gorgeous houses (and in recent years an ever-larger number of places to spend money), it's sometimes burdened with the moniker "Prague's most beautiful street." A tiny passageway at No. 13, on the left-hand side as you go up, leads to Tržištěulice and the **Schönbornský palác** ㉖, once Franz Kafka's home, now the embassy of the United States. Tržiště winds down to the quarter's traffic-plagued main street, Karmelitská, where the famous Infant Jesus of Prague resides in the **Kostel Panny Marie vítězné.** A few doors away, closer to

Tržiště, is a quiet oasis, the **Vrtbovská zahrada** ㉗. Tiny Prokopská ulice leads off of Karmelitská, past the former Church of St. Procopius (now converted, oddly, into an apartment block), and into Maltézské náměstí (Maltese Square), a characteristically noble compound. The square next door, **Velkopřevorské náměstí**, boasts even grander palaces.

A tiny bridge at the cramped square's lower end takes you across the creeklike Čertovka to the island of **Kampa** ㉘ and its broad lawns, cafés, and river views. Winding your way underneath Karlův most and along the street U lužického semináře brings you to a quiet walled garden, **Vojanovy sady** ㉙. To the northwest, hiding off busy Letenská ulice near the Malostranská metro station, is **Zahrada Valdštejnského paláce** ㉚, a more formal garden with an unbeatable view of Prague Castle looming above.

TIMING

The area is at its best in the evening, when the softer light hides the crumbling facades and brings you into a world of glimmering beauty. The basic walk described here could take as little as half a day—longer if you'd like to explore the area's lovely nooks and crannies.

Sights to See

★ ㉔ **CHRÁM SVATÉHO MIKULÁŠE** (Church of St. Nicholas). With its dynamic curves, this church is one of the purest and most ambitious examples of high Baroque. The celebrated architect Christoph Dientzenhofer began the Jesuit church in 1704 on the site of one of the more active Hussite churches of 15th-century Prague. Work on the building was taken over by his son Kilian Ignaz Dientzenhofer, who built the dome and presbytery. Anselmo Lurago completed the whole in 1755 by adding the bell tower. The juxtaposition of the broad, full-bodied dome with the slender bell tower is one of the many striking architectural contrasts that mark the Prague skyline. Inside, the vast pink-and-green space is impossible to take in with a single glance. Every corner bristles with movement, guiding the eye first to the dramatic statues, then to the hectic frescoes, and on to the shining faux-marble pillars. Many of the statues are the work of Ignaz Platzer, and in fact they constitute his last blaze of success. Platzer's workshop was forced to declare bankruptcy when the centralizing and secularizing reforms of Joseph II toward the end of the 18th century brought an end to the flamboyant Baroque era. *Malostranské nám. 30 Kč. Daily 9–4.*

❷❽ KAMPA. Prague's largest island is cut off from the "mainland" by the narrow Čertovka streamlet. The name Čertovka, or Devil's Stream, reputedly refers to a cranky old lady who once lived on Maltese Square (given the river's present filthy state, the name is certainly appropriate). The unusually well-kept lawns of the **Kampa Gardens** that occupy much of the island are one of the few places in Prague where sitting on the grass is openly tolerated. If it's a warm day, spread out a blanket and bask for a while in the sunshine. The row of benches that lines the river is also a popular spot from which to contemplate the city. At night this stretch along the river is especially romantic.

★ ❷❷ KARLÙV MOST (Charles Bridge). The view from the foot of the bridge on the Old Town side is nothing short of breathtaking, encompassing the towers and domes of the Lesser Quarter and the soaring spires of St. Vitus's Cathedral to the northwest. This heavenly vision changes subtly in perspective as you walk across the bridge, attended by the host of Baroque saints that decorate the bridge's peaceful Gothic stones. At night its drama is spellbinding: St. Vitus's Cathedral lit in a ghostly green, the castle in monumental yellow, and the Church of St. Nicholas in a voluptuous pink, all viewed through the menacing silhouettes of the bowed statues and the Gothic towers. If you do nothing else in Prague, you must visit the Charles Bridge at night. During the day the pedestrian bridge buzzes with activity. Street musicians vie with artisans hawking jewelry, paintings, and glass for the hearts and wallets of the passing multitude. At night the crowds thin out a little, the musicians multiply, and the bridge becomes a long block party—nearly everyone brings a bottle.

When the Přemyslid princes set up residence in Prague in the 10th century, there was a ford across the Vltava at this point—a vital link along one of Europe's major trading routes. After several wooden bridges and the first stone bridge had washed away in floods, Charles IV appointed the 27-year-old German Peter Parler, the architect of St. Vitus's Cathedral, to build a new structure in 1357. After 1620, following the defeat of Czech Protestants by Catholic Hapsburgs at the Battle of White Mountain, the bridge became a symbol of the Counter-Reformation's vigorous re-Catholicization efforts. The many Baroque statues that began to appear in the late 17th century, commissioned by Catholics, eventually came to symbolize the totality of the Austrian (hence Catholic) triumph. The Czech writer Milan Kundera sees the statues from this perspective: "The thousands of saints looking out from all sides, threatening you, following you, hypnotizing you, are the raging hordes of occupiers who invaded Bohemia 350 years ago to tear the people's faith and language from their hearts."

The religious conflict is less obvious nowadays, leaving only the artistic tension between Baroque and Gothic that gives the bridge its allure. It's worth pausing to take a closer look at some of the statues as you walk toward the Lesser Quarter. The third on the right, a bronze crucifix from the mid-17th century, is the oldest of all. It is mounted on the location of a wooden cross destroyed in a battle with the Swedes (the golden Hebrew inscription was reputedly financed by a Jew accused of defiling the cross). Eighth on the right, the statue of St. John of Nepomuk, designed by Johann Brokoff in 1683, begins the Baroque lineup of saints. On the left-hand side, sticking out from the bridge between the 9th and 10th statues (the latter has a wonderfully expressive vanquished Satan), stands a Roland (Bruncvík) statue. This knightly figure, bearing the coat of arms of the Old Town, was once a reminder that this part of the bridge belonged to the Old Town before Prague became a unified city in 1784.

In the eyes of most art historians, the most valuable statue is the 12th on the left, near the Lesser Quarter end. Mathias Braun's statue of St. Luitgarde depicts the blind saint kissing Christ's wounds. The most compelling grouping, however, is the second from the end on the left, a work of Ferdinand Maxmilian Brokoff (son of Johann) from 1714. Here the saints are incidental; the main attraction is the Turk, his face expressing extreme boredom at guarding the Christians imprisoned in the cage at his side. When the statue was erected, just 31 years after the second Turkish siege of Vienna, it scandalized the Prague public, who smeared it with mud. A half-dozen of the 30 bridge sculptures are 19th-century replacements for originals damaged in wars or sunk in a 1784 flood. All but a couple of the bridge's surviving Baroque statues, including St. Luitgarde and the Turk, have been replaced by modern copies. The 17th- and 18th-century originals are in safer quarters, protected from Prague's acidic air. Several, including St. Luitgarde, can be viewed in the Lapidarium museum at the Výstaviště exhibition grounds in Prague 7; a few more occupy a man-made cavern at Vyšehrad (☞ Nové Město [New Town] and Vyšehrad, *below*).

KOSTEL PANNY MARIE VÍTĚZNÉ (Church of Our Lady Victorious). This comfortably ramshackle church on the Lesser Quarter's main street is the unlikely home of one of Prague's best-known religious artifacts, the Pražské Jezulátko (Infant Jesus of Prague). Originally brought to Prague from Spain in the 16th century, this tiny porcelain doll (now bathed in neon lighting) is renowned worldwide for showering miracles on anyone willing to kneel before it and pray. Nuns from a nearby convent arrive at dawn each day to change the infant's clothes; pieces of the doll's extensive wardrobe have been sent by believers from around the world. *Karmelitská 9A. Free. Mon.–Sat. 10–5:30, Sun. 1–5.*

LEDEBURSKÁ ZAHRADA (Ledeburg Garden). Rows of steeply banked Baroque gardens rise behind the palaces of Valdštejnská ulice. This one makes a pleasant spot for a rest amid shady arbors and niches. The garden, with its frescoes and statuary, was restored with support from a fund headed by Czech president Václav Havel and Charles, Prince of Wales. *Entrance at Valdštejnské nám. 3; also from the south gardens of Prague Castle in summer. 25 Kč. Daily 10–6.*

㉓ **MALOSTRANSKÉ NÁMĚSTÍ** (Lesser Quarter Square). The arcaded houses on the east and south sides of the square, dating from the 16th and 17th centuries, exhibit a mix of Baroque and Renaissance elements. The Czech Parliament resides partly in the gaudy yellow-and-green palace on the square's north side, partly in the street behind the palace Sněmovní. The huge bulk of the Church of St. Nicholas divides the lower, busier section—buzzing with restaurants, street vendors, clubs, and shops—from the quieter, upper part.

㉕ **NERUDOVA ULICE.** This steep little street used to be the last leg of the Royal Way walked by the king before his coronation, and it is still the best way to get to Prague Castle. It was named for the 19th-century Czech journalist and poet Jan Neruda (after whom Chilean poet Pablo Neruda renamed himself). Until Joseph II's administrative reforms in the late 18th century, house numbering was unknown in Prague. Each house bore a name, depicted on the facade, and these are particularly prominent on Nerudova ulice. House No. 6, **U červeného orla** (At the Red Eagle), proudly displays a faded painting of a red eagle. No. 12 is known as **U tří housliček** (At the Three Fiddles). In the early 18th century, three generations of the Edlinger violin-making family lived here. Joseph II's scheme numbered each house according to its position in its "town" (here the Lesser Quarter) rather than its sequence on the street. The red plates record the original house numbers; the blue ones are the numbers used in addresses today. Many architectural guides refer to the old, red-number plates, which may confuse tourists.

Two palaces break the unity of the burghers' houses on Nerudova ulice. Both were designed by the adventurous Baroque architect Giovanni Santini, one of the Italian builders most in demand by wealthy nobles of the early 18th century. The **Morzin Palace,** on the left at No. 5, is now the Romanian Embassy. The fascinating facade, with an allegory of night and day, was created in 1713 and is the work of Ferdinand Brokoff of Charles Bridge statue fame. Across the street at No. 20 is the **Thun-Hohenstein Palace,** now the Italian Embassy. The gateway with two enormous eagles (the emblem of the Kolovrat family, who owned the building at the time) is the work of the other great Charles Bridge statue sculptor, Mathias Braun. Santini himself lived at No. 14, the **Valkoun House.**

The archway at Nerudova 13 hides one of the many winding passageways that give the Lesser Quarter its enchantingly ghostly character at night. Higher up the street at No. 33 is the **Bretfeld Palace,** a rococo house on the corner of Jánský vršek. The relief of St. Nicholas on the facade is the work of Ignaz Platzer, a sculptor known for his classic and rococo work, but the building is valued more for its historical associations than for its architecture: this is where Mozart, his lyricist partner Lorenzo da Ponte, and the aging but still infamous philanderer and music lover Casanova stayed at the time of the world premiere of *Don Giovanni* in 1787.

NEED A BREAK? Nerudova ulice is filled with little restaurants and snack bars and offers something for everyone. **U zeleného čaje** (Nerudova 19) is a fragrant little tearoom offering herbal and fruit teas as well as light salads and sweets. **U Kocoura** (Nerudova 2) is a traditional pub that hasn't caved in to touristic niceties.

SCHÖNBORNSKÝ PALÁC (Schönborn Palace). Franz Kafka had an apartment in this massive Baroque building at the top of Tržištěulice in mid-1917, after moving from Zlatá ulička, or Golden Lane (☞ Pražský hrad [Prague Castle], *below*). The U.S. Embassy now occupies this prime location. If you look through the gates, you can see the beautiful formal gardens rising up to the Petřín hill. Unfortunately, they are not open to the public, but can be glimpsed from the neighboring garden, Vrtbovská zahrada (☞ *below*). Tržiště *at Vlašská.*

STAROMĚSTSKÁ MOSTECKÁ VĚŽ (Old Town Bridge Tower). This was where Peter Parler, the architect of St. Vitus's Cathedral and eventually the Charles Bridge, began his bridge building. The carved facades he designed for the sides of the tower were destroyed by Swedish soldiers in 1648, at the end of the Thirty Years' War. The sculptures facing the Old Town, however, are still intact (although some are recent copies); they depict an old and gout-ridden Charles IV with his son, who later became Wenceslas IV. Above them are two of Bohemia's patron saints, Adalbert of Prague and Sigismund. Inside the tower is a small exhibit of antique musical instruments. 20 *Kč. Daily* 10–5 *(until* 7 *in summer).*

VELKOPŘEVORSKÉ NÁMĚSTÍ (Grand Priory Square). This square lies just south of the Charles Bridge, next to the Čertovka. The Grand Prior's Palace fronting the square is considered one of the finest Baroque buildings in the Lesser Quarter, though it is now part of the Embassy of the Knights of Malta and no longer open to the public. Opposite is the flamboyant orange-and-white stucco facade of the Buquoy Palace, built in 1719 by Giovanni Santini and the present home of the French Embassy. The so-called **John Lennon Peace Wall**, leading to a bridge over the Čertovka, was once a kind of monument to youthful rebellion, emblazoned with a large painted head of the former Beatle, lyrics from his songs, and other messages of peace. It has lost much social significance, not to mention attractiveness, since the years around the 1989 revolution when graffiti actually meant something in Prague.

29 VOJANOVY SADY (Vojan Park). Once the gardens of the Monastery of the Discalced Carmelites, later taken over by the Order of the English Virgins, and now part of the Ministry of Finance, this walled garden, with its weeping willows, fruit trees, and benches, makes another peaceful haven in summer. Exhibitions of modern sculptures are often held here, contrasting sharply with the two Baroque chapels and the graceful Ignaz Platzer statue of John of Nepomuk standing on a fish at the entrance. The park is surrounded by the high walls of the old monastery and new Ministry of Finance buildings, with only an occasional glimpse of a tower or spire to remind you that you're in Prague. *U lužického semináře, between Letenská ul. and Míšeňská ul. Nov.–Mar., daily 8–5; Apr.–Oct., daily 8–7.*

★ 27 VRTBOVSKÁ ZAHRADA (Vrtba Garden). An unobtrusive door on noisy Karmelitská hides the entranceway to a fascinating oasis that also has one of the best views over the Lesser Quarter. The street door opens onto the intimate courtyard of the Vrtbovský palác (Vrtba Palace), which is now private housing. Two Renaissance wings flank the courtyard; the left one was built in 1575, the right one in 1591. The owner of the latter house was one of the 27 Bohemian nobles executed by the Hapsburgs in 1621 before the Old Town Hall. The house was given as confiscated property to Count Sezima of Vrtba, who bought the neighboring property and turned the buildings into a late-Renaissance palace. The Vrtba Garden, created a century later, reopened in summer 1998 after an excruciatingly long renovation. This is the most elegant of the Lesser Quarter's public gardens, built in five levels rising behind the courtyard in a wave of statuary-bedecked staircases and formal terraces to reach a seashell-decorated pavilion at the top. (The fenced-off garden immediately behind and above belongs to the U.S. Embassy.) The powerful stone figure of Atlas that caps the entranceway in the courtyard and most of the other classically derived statues are from the workshop of Mathias Braun, perhaps the best of the Czech Baroque sculptors. *Karmelitská 25. 20 Kč. Apr.–Oct., daily 10–6.*

....

OFF THE BEATEN PATH **VILLA BERTRAMKA** – Mozart fans won't want to pass up a visit to this villa, where the great composer lived during a couple of his visits to Prague. The small, well-organized W. A. Mozart Museum is packed with memorabilia, including a flyer for a performance of *Don Giovanni* in 1788, only months after the opera's world premiere at the Estates Theater. Also on hand is one of the master's pianos. Take Tram No. 12 from Karmelitská south (or ride Metro Line B) to the Anděl metro station, then transfer to Tram No. 4, 7, 9, or 10 and ride to the first stop (Bertramka). A 10-minute walk, following the signs, brings you to the villa. *Mozartova ul. 169, Prague 5 (Smíchov), tel. 02/540–012. 90 Kč. Apr.–Oct., daily 9:30–6; Nov.–Mar., daily 9:30–5.*

....

★ ③⓪ **ZAHRADA VALDŠTEJNSKÉHO PALÁCE** (Wallenstein Palace Gardens). Albrecht von Wallenstein, onetime owner of the house and gardens, began a meteoric military career in 1622 when the Austrian emperor Ferdinand II retained him to save the empire from the Swedes and Protestants during the Thirty Years' War. Wallenstein, wealthy by marriage, offered to raise 20,000 men at his own cost and lead them personally. Ferdinand II accepted and showered Wallenstein with confiscated land and titles. Wallenstein's first acquisition was this enormous area. Having knocked down 23 houses, a brick factory, and three gardens, in 1623 he began to build his magnificent palace with its idiosyncratic high-walled gardens and superb, vaulted Renaissance *sala terrena* (room opening onto a garden). Walking around the formal paths, you'll come across numerous statues, an unusual fountain with a woman spouting water from her breasts, and a lava-stone grotto along the wall. Most of the palace itself now serves the Czech Senate as meeting chamber and offices. The palace's cavernous former Jízdárna, or riding school, now hosts occasional art exhibitions. *Garden entrance: Letenská 10. Garden free. Garden May–Sept., daily 9–7; Mar. 21–Apr. 30, and Oct., daily 10–6.*

HRADČANY (CASTLE AREA)

To the west of Prague Castle is the residential Hradčany (Castle Area), the town that during the early 14th century emerged out of a collection of monasteries and churches. The concentration of history packed into Prague Castle and Hradčany challenges visitors not versed in the ups and downs of Bohemian kings, religious uprisings, wars, and oppression. The picturesque area surrounding Prague Castle, with its breathtaking vistas of the Old Town and the Lesser Quarter, is ideal for just wandering. But the castle itself, with its convoluted history and architecture, is difficult to appreciate fully without investing a little more time.

A Good Walk

Begin on Nerudova ulice (☞ Karlův most [Charles Bridge] and Malá Strana [Lesser Quarter], *above*), which runs east–west a few hundred yards south of Prague Castle. At the western (upper) end of the street, look for a flight of stone steps guarded by two saintly statues. Take the stairs up to Loretánská ulice, and take in panoramic views of the Church of St. Nicholas and the Lesser Quarter. At the top of the steps, turn left and walk a couple hundred yards until you come to a dusty elongated square named Pohořelec (Scene of Fire), which suffered tragic fires in 1420, 1541, and 1741. Go through the inconspicuous gateway at No. 8 and up the steps, and you'll find yourself in the courtyard of one of the city's richest monasteries, the **Strahovský klášter** ③.

Retrace your steps to Loretánské náměstí, the square at the head of Loretánská ulice that is flanked by the feminine curves of the Baroque church **Loreta** ③. Across the road, the 29 half pillars of the Černínský palác (Černín Palace) now mask the Czech Ministry of Foreign Affairs. At the bottom of Loretánské náměstí, a little lane trails to the left into the area known as **Nový Svět**; the name means "New World," though the district is as old-world as they come. Turn right onto the street Nový Svět. Around the corner you get a tantalizing view of the cathedral through the trees. Walk down the winding Kanovnická ulice past the Austrian Embassy and the dignified but melancholy Kostel svatého Jana Nepomuckého (Church of St. John of Nepomuk). At the top of the street on the left, the rounded, Renaissance corner house, Martinický palác, catches the eye with its detailed sgraffiti decorations. Martinický palác opens onto **Hradčanské náměstí** ㉝ with its grandiose gathering of Renaissance and Baroque palaces. To the left of the bright yellow Arcibiskupský palác (Archbishop's Palace) on the square is an alleyway leading down to the **Národní galerie** ㉞ and its collections of European art. Across the square, the handsome sgraffito sweep of **Schwarzenberský palác** ㉟ beckons; this is the building you saw from the back side at the beginning of the tour.

TIMING

To do justice to the subtle charms of Hradčany, allow at least an hour just for ambling and admiring the passing buildings and views of the city. The Strahovský klášter halls need about a half hour to take in, more if you tour the small picture gallery there, and the Loreta and its treasures need at least that length of time. The Národní galerie in the Šternberský palác deserves at least a couple of hours. Keep in mind that several places are not open on Monday.

Sights to See

㉝ **HRADČANSKÉ NÁMĚSTÍ** (Hradčany Square). With its fabulous mixture of Baroque and Renaissance housing, topped by the castle itself, the square had a prominent role (disguised, ironically, as Vienna) in the film *Amadeus*, directed by the then-exiled Czech director Miloš Forman. The house at No. 7 was the set for Mozart's residence, where the composer was haunted by the masked figure he thought was his father. Forman used the flamboyant rococo **Arcibiskupský palác** (Archbishop's Palace), on the left as you face the castle, as the Viennese archbishop's palace. The plush interior, shown off in the film, is open to the public only on Maundy Thursday (the Thursday before Easter). No. 11 was home for a brief time after World War II to a little girl named Marie Jana Korbelová, who would grow up to be U.S. Secretary of State Madeleine Albright.

32 **LORETA** (Loreto Church). The church's seductive lines were a conscious move on the part of Counter-Reformation Jesuits in the 17th century who wanted to build up the cult of Mary and attract the largely Protestant Bohemians back to the church. According to legend, angels had carried Mary's house from Nazareth and dropped it in a patch of laurel trees in Ancona, Italy. Known as *Loreto* (from the Latin for laurel), it immediately became a center of pilgrimage. The Prague Loreto was one of many symbolic reenactments of this scene across Europe, and it worked: pilgrims came in droves. The graceful facade, with its voluptuous tower, was built in 1720 by Kilian Ignaz Dientzenhofer, the architect of the two St. Nicholas churches in Prague. Most spectacular of all is a small exhibition upstairs displaying the religious treasures presented to Mary in thanks for various services, including a monstrance studded with 6,500 diamonds. *Loretánské nám. 7. 80 Kč (priests, monks, and nuns admitted free). Tues.–Sun. 9–12:15 and 1–4:30.*

★ 34 **NÁRODNÍ GALERIE** (National Gallery). Housed in the 18th-century **Šternberský palác** (Sternberg Palace), this collection, though impressive, is limited compared to German and Austrian holdings. During the time when Berlin, Dresden, and Vienna were building up superlative old-master galleries, Prague languished, neglected by her Viennese rulers—one reason why the city's museums lag behind. On the first floor there's an exhibition of icons, Italian religious art from the 3rd to 14th centuries, and early Dutch Renaissance masters. Up a second flight of steps is an assortment of paintings by Cranach, Holbein,

Dürer, Van Dyck, El Greco, Rembrandt, and Rubens. Other branches of the National Gallery are scattered around town. *Hradčanské nám. 15, tel. 02/2051–4634. 90 Kč. Tues.–Sun. 10–6. www.ngprague.cz*

NOVÝ SVĚT. This picturesque, winding little alley, with facades from the 17th and 18th centuries, once housed Prague's poorest residents; now many of the homes are used as artists' studios. The last house on the street, No. 1, was the home of the Danish-born astronomer Tycho Brahe. Living so close to the Loreto, so the story goes, Tycho was constantly disturbed during his nightly stargazing by the church bells. He ended up complaining to his patron, Emperor Rudolf II, who instructed the Capuchin monks to finish their services before the first star appeared in the sky.

㉟ SCHWARZENBERSKÝ PALÁC (Schwarzenberg Palace). This boxy palace with its extravagant sgraffito facade contains the **Vojenské historické muzeum** (Military History Museum), one of the largest of its kind in Europe. A dim, old-fashioned collection, it concentrates on pre-20th-century Czech military history. Of more general interest are the jousting tournaments held in the courtyard in summer. *Hradčanské nám. 2. 20 Kč. Apr.–Oct., Tues.–Sun. 10–6.*

★ ㉛ STRAHOVSKÝ KLÁŠTER (Strahov Monastery). Founded by the Premonstratensian order in 1140, the monastery remained in its hands until 1952, when the Communists suppressed all religious orders and turned the entire complex into the **Památník národního písemnictví** (Museum of National Literature). The major building of interest is the **Strahov Library,** with its collection of early Czech manuscripts, the 10th-century Strahov New Testament, and the collected works of famed Danish astronomer Tycho Brahe. Also of note is the late-18th-century **Philosophical Hall.** Engulfing its ceilings is a startling sky blue fresco that depicts an unusual cast of characters, including Socrates' nagging wife Xanthippe, Greek astronomer Thales with his trusty telescope, and a collection of Greek philosophers mingling with Descartes, Diderot, and

Voltaire. Also on the premises is the order's small art gallery, highlighted by late-Gothic altars and paintings from Rudolf II's time. You can arrange for a tour in English with several days' advance notice. *Strahovské nádvoří 1/132, tel. 02/2051–6671 (tour arrangements). Gallery 25 Kč, library tour 20 Kč. Gallery Tues.–Sun. 9–noon and 12:30–5. Library daily 9–noon and 1–5. www.vol.cz/monastery/infoeng1*

OFF THE BEATEN PATH **PETŘÍN** – For a superb view of the city—from a mostly undiscovered, tourist-free perch—stroll over from the Strahov Monastery along the paths toward Prague's own miniature version of the Eiffel Tower. You'll find yourself in a hilltop park, laced with footpaths, with several buildings clustered together near the tower—just keep going gradually upward until you reach the tower's base. The tower and its breathtaking view, the mirror maze (*bludiště*) in a small structure near the tower's base, and the seemingly abandoned svatý Vavřinec (St. Lawrence) church are beautifully peaceful and well worth an afternoon's wandering. You can also walk up from Karmelitská ulice or Újezd down in the Lesser Quarter or ride the funicular railway from U lanové dráhy ulice, off Újezd. Regular public-transportation tickets are valid. For the descent, take the funicular or meander on foot down through the stations of the cross on the pathways leading back to the Lesser Quarter.

PRAŽSKÝ HRAD (PRAGUE CASTLE)

Numbers in the text correspond to numbers in the margin and on the Prague Castle (Pražský hrad) map.

Despite its monolithic presence, the Prague Castle is a collection of buildings dating from the 10th to the 20th century, all linked by internal courtyards. The most important structures are **Chrám svatého Víta** ㊾, clearly visible soaring above the castle walls, and the **Královský palác** ㊿, the official residence of kings and presidents and still the center of political power in the Czech Republic. The castle is compact and easy to navigate. Be forewarned: in summer, Chrám svatého Víta and Zlatá ulička take the brunt of the heavy sightseeing traffic, although all of the castle is hugely popular.

TIMING

The castle is at its mysterious best in early morning and late evening, and it is incomparable when it snows. The cathedral deserves an hour, as does the Královský palác, while you can easily spend an entire day taking in the museums, the views of the city, and the hidden nooks of the castle. Remember that some sights, such as the Lobkovický palác and the National Gallery branch at Klášter svatého Jiří, are not open on Monday.

Sights to See

55 BAZILIKA SVATÉHO JIŘÍ (St. George's Basilica). This church was originally built in the 10th century by Prince Vratislav I, the father of Prince (and St.) Wenceslas. It was dedicated to St. George (of dragon fame), who it was believed would be more agreeable to the still largely pagan people. The outside was remodeled during early Baroque times, although the striking rusty red color is in keeping with the look of the Romanesque edifice. The interior looks more or less as it did in the 12th century and is the best-preserved Romanesque relic in the country. The effect is at once barnlike and peaceful, the warm golden yellow of the stone walls and the small arched windows exuding a sense of enduring harmony. The house-shape painted tomb at the front of the church holds the remains of the founder, Vratislav I. Up the steps, in a chapel to the right, is the tomb Peter Parler designed for St. Ludmila, the grandmother of St. Wenceslas. For admission information, *see* Informační středisko, *below. Nám. U sv. Jiří. Apr.– Oct., daily 9–5; Nov.–Mar., daily 9–4.*

★ **53 CHRÁM SVATÉHO VÍTA** (St. Vitus's Cathedral). With its graceful, soaring towers, this Gothic cathedral—among the most beautiful

pražký hrad (prague castle)

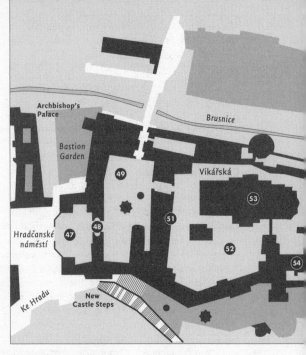

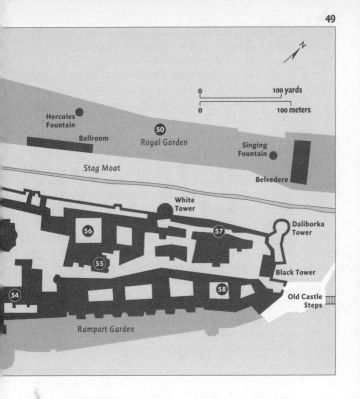

0   100 yards
0   100 meters

Hercules
Fountain

Ballroom

Royal Garden

50

Singing
Fountain

Stag Moat

Belvedere

White
Tower

56

57

Daliborka
Tower

55

Black Tower

54

58

Old Castle
Steps

Rampart Garden

in Europe—is the spiritual heart not only of Prague Castle, but of the entire country. It has a long and complicated history, beginning in the 10th century and continuing to its completion in 1929. If you want to hear its history in depth, English-speaking guided tours of the cathedral and the Královský palác (☞ *below*) can be arranged at the information office across from the cathedral entrance.

Once you enter the cathedral, pause to take in the vast but delicate beauty of the Gothic and neo-Gothic interior glowing in the colorful light that filters through the startlingly brilliant stained-glass windows. This western third of the structure, including the facade and the two towers you can see from outside, was not completed until 1929, following the initiative of the Union for the Completion of the Cathedral, set up in the last days of the 19th century. Don't let the neo-Gothic illusion keep you from examining this new section. The six stained-glass windows to your left and right and the large rose window behind are modern masterpieces. Take a good look at the third window up on the left. The familiar Art Nouveau flamboyance, depicting the blessing of Sts. Cyril and Methodius (9th-century missionaries to the Slavs and creators of the Cyrillic alphabet), is the work of the Czech father of the style, Alfons Mucha. He achieved the subtle coloring by painting rather than staining the glass.

If you walk halfway up the right-hand aisle, you will find the **Svatováclavská kaple** (Chapel of St. Wenceslas). With a tomb holding the saint's remains, walls covered in semiprecious stones, and paintings depicting the life of Wenceslas, this square chapel is the ancient heart of the cathedral. Stylistically, it represents a high point of the dense, richly decorated though rather gloomy Gothic favored by Charles IV and his successors. Wenceslas (the "good king" of Christmas-carol fame) was a determined Christian in an era of widespread paganism. Around 925, as prince of Bohemia, he founded a rotunda church dedicated to St. Vitus on this site. But the prince's brother, Boleslav, was impatient to take power, and he ambushed Wenceslas in 929 (or 935 according to some experts) near a church at Stará Boleslav, northeast of Prague. Wenceslas was originally buried in that church, but his grave produced so many miracles that he rapidly became a symbol of piety for the common people, something that greatly irritated the new Prince Boleslav. Boleslav was finally forced to honor his brother by reburying the body in the St. Vitus Rotunda. Shortly afterward, Wenceslas was canonized.

The rotunda was replaced by a Romanesque basilica in the late 11th century. Work was begun on the existing building in 1344. For the first few years the chief architect was the Frenchman Mathias d'Arras, but after his death in 1352 the work was continued by the 22-year-old German architect Peter Parler, who went on to build the Charles Bridge and many other Prague treasures.

The small door in the back of the chapel leads to the **Korunní komora** (Crown Chamber), the repository of the Bohemian crown jewels. It remains locked with seven keys held by seven different people and is definitely not open to the public.

A little beyond the Chapel of St. Wenceslas on the same side, stairs lead down to the underground **royal crypt,** interesting primarily for the information it provides about the cathedral's history. As you descend the stairs, you'll see parts of the old Romanesque basilica and portions of the foundations of the rotunda. Moving around into the second room, you'll find a rather eclectic group of royal remains ensconced in new sarcophagi dating from the 1930s. In the center is Charles IV, who died in 1378. Rudolf II, patron of Renaissance Prague, is entombed at the rear in the original tin coffin. To his right is Maria Amalia, the only child of Empress Maria Theresa to reside in Prague. Ascending the wooden steps back into the cathedral, you'll come to the white-marble **Kralovské mausoleum** (Royal

Mausoleum), atop which lie stone statues of the first two Hapsburg kings to rule in Bohemia, Ferdinand I and Maximilian II, and of Ferdinand's consort, Anne Jagiello.

The cathedral's **Kralovské oratorium** (Royal Oratory) was used by the kings and their families when attending mass. Built in 1493, the work is a perfect example of late Gothic, laced on the outside with a stone network of gnarled branches very similar in pattern to the ceiling vaulting in the Královský palác (☞ *below*). The oratory is connected to the palace by an elevated, covered walkway, which you can see from outside.

A few more steps toward the east end, you can't fail to catch sight of the ornate silver **sarcophagus of St. John of Nepomuk**. According to legend, when Nepomuk's body was exhumed in 1721 to be reinterred, the tongue was found to be still intact and pumping with blood. This strange tale served a highly political purpose. The Catholic Church and the Hapsburgs were seeking a new folk hero to replace the Protestant forerunner Jan Hus, whom they despised. The 14th-century priest Nepomuk, killed during a power struggle with King Václav IV, was sainted and reburied a few years later with great ceremony in the 3,700-pound silver tomb, replete with angels and cherubim; the tongue was enshrined in its own reliquary.

The eight chapels around the back of the cathedral are the work of the original architect, Mathias d'Arras. A number of old tombstones, including some badly worn grave markers of medieval royalty, can be seen within, amid furnishings from later periods. Opposite the wooden relief, depicting the looting of the cathedral by Protestants in 1619, is the **Valdštejnská kaple** (Wallenstein Chapel). Since the last century, the chapel has housed the Gothic tombstones of its two architects, d'Arras and Peter Parler, who died in 1352 and 1399, respectively. If you look up to the balcony, you can just make out the busts of these two men, designed by Parler's workshop. The other busts around the triforium depict royalty and other VIPs of the time.

ONE LAST TRAVEL TIP:

Pack an easy way to reach the world.

123 456 7891 2345
J.D. SMITH

Wherever you travel, the MCI WorldCom Card℠ is the easiest way to stay in touch. You can use it to call to and from more than 125 countries worldwide. And you can earn bonus miles every time you use your card. So go ahead, travel the world. MCI WorldCom℠ makes it even more rewarding. For additional access codes, visit **www.wcom.com/worldphone**.

MCI WORLDCOM.

EASY TO CALL WORLDWIDE

1. Just dial the WorldPhone® access number of the country you're calling from.

2. Dial or give the operator your MCI WorldCom Card number.

3. Dial or give the number you're calling.

Belgium ◆	0800-10012
Czech Republic ◆	00-42-000112
Denmark ◆	8001-0022
France ◆	0-800-99-0019
Germany	0800-888-8000
Hungary ◆	06▼-800-01411
Ireland	1-800-55-1001
Italy ◆	172-1022
Mexico	01-800-021-8000
Netherlands ◆	0800-022-91-22
Spain	900-99-0014
Switzerland ◆	0800-89-0222
United Kingdom	0800-89-0222
United States	1-800-888-8000

◆ Public phones may require deposit of coin or phone card for dial tone. ▼ Wait for second dial tone.

EARN FREQUENT FLIER MILES

Bureau de change

Cambio

外国為替

In this city, you can find money on almost any street.

NO-FEE FOREIGN EXCHANGE

The Chase Manhattan Bank has over 80 convenient
locations near New York City destinations such as:

Times Square
Rockefeller Center
Empire State Building
2 World Trade Center
United Nations Plaza

Exchange any of 75 foreign currencies

◻ CHASE

THE RIGHT RELATIONSHIP IS EVERYTHING.®

The Hussite wars in the 15th century put an end to the first phase of the cathedral's construction. During the short era of illusory peace before the Thirty Years' War, the massive south tower was completed, but lack of money quashed any idea of finishing the building, and the cathedral was closed by a wall built across from the Chapel of St. Wenceslas. Not until the 20th century was the western side of the cathedral, with its two towers, completed in the spirit of Parler's conception.

A key element of the cathedral's teeming, rich exterior decoration is the **Last Judgment mosaic** above the ceremonial entrance, called the Golden Portal, on the south side. The use of mosaic is quite rare in countries north of the Alps; this work, dating from the 1370s, is made of one million glass and stone chunks. It's currently undergoing an extensive, desperately needed restoration led by the Getty Conservation Institute. The central field shows Christ in glory, adored by Charles IV and his consort, Elizabeth of Pomerania, as well as several saints; the risen dead and attendant angels are on the left; and on the right the flames of Hell lick around the figure of Satan. *St. Vitus's Cathedral. Western section free; chapels, crypt, and tower accessible with castle-wide ticket (see Informační středisko, below). Apr.–Oct., daily 9–5; Nov.–Mar., daily 9–4.*

➍➒ **DRUHÉ NÁDVOŘÍ** (Second Courtyard). Empress Maria Theresa's court architect, Nicolò Pacassi, received the imperial approval to remake the castle in the 1760s, as it was badly damaged by Prussian shelling during the Seven Years' War in 1757. The Second Courtyard was the main victim of Pacassi's attempts at imparting classical grandeur to what had been a picturesque collection of Gothic and Renaissance styles. Except for the view of the spires of St. Vitus's Cathedral, the exterior courtyard offers little for the eye to feast upon. This courtyard also houses the rather gaudy **Kaple svatého Kříže** (Chapel of the Holy Cross), with decorations from the 18th and 19th centuries.

Built in the late 16th and early 17th century, the Second Courtyard was originally part of a reconstruction program commissioned by Rudolf II, under whom Prague enjoyed a period of unparalleled cultural development. Once the Prague court was established, the emperor gathered around him some of the world's best craftsmen, artists, and scientists, including the brilliant astronomers Johannes Kepler and Tycho Brahe.

Rudolf also amassed a large and famed collection of fine and decorative art, scientific instruments, philosophic and alchemical books, natural wonders, coins, and everything else under the sun. The bulk of the collection was looted by the Swedes during the Thirty Years' War, removed to Vienna when the imperial capital returned there after Rudolf's death, or auctioned off during the 18th century. Artworks that survived the turmoil, for the most part acquired after Rudolf's time, are displayed in the **Obrazárna** (Picture Gallery), on the left side of the courtyard as you face St. Vitus's. In rooms elegantly redecorated by the official castle architect, Bořek Šípek, there are good Renaissance, Mannerist, and Baroque paintings that hint at the luxurious tastes of Rudolf's court. Across the passageway by the gallery entrance is the **Císařská konírna** (Imperial Stable), where temporary exhibitions are held. The passageway forms the northern entrance to the castle and leads out over a luxurious ravine known as the **Jelení příkop** (Stag Moat), which can be entered (from April through October) either here or at the lower end via the metal catwalk off Chotkova ulice. *Obrazárna: Second Courtyard. 100 Kč. Daily 10–6.*

🔟 INFORMAČNÍ STŘEDISKO (Castle Information Office). This is the place to come for entrance tickets, guided tours, headphones for listening to recorded tours in English, tickets to cultural events held at the castle, and money changing. Tickets are valid for three consecutive days and allow admission to the older parts of St. Vitus's Cathedral, Královský palác, St. George's Basilica (but not the adjacent National Gallery exhibition), and a medieval bastion called Mihulka with an exhibition on alchemy. These sights may be visited only with the three-day ticket; the 20th-century section of the cathedral is free. Buy tickets to other castle sights at the door. If you just want to walk through the castle grounds, note that the gates close at midnight from April through October and at 11 PM the rest of the year, while the gardens are open from April through October only. *Třetí nádvoří, across from the entrance to St. Vitus's Cathedral, tel. 02/2437–3368. 3-day tickets 120 Kč; English-language guided tours 300 Kč for up to 5 people, 60 Kč per additional person (advance booking recommended); grounds and gardens free. Apr.–Oct., daily 9–5; Nov.–Mar., daily 9–4.*

56 **KLÁŠTER SVATÉHO JIŘÍ** (St. George's Convent). The first convent in Bohemia was founded here in 973 next to the even older St. George's Basilica (☞ *above*). The National Gallery collections of Czech Mannerist and Baroque art are housed here. The highlights include the voluptuous work of Rudolf II's court painters, the giant Baroque religious statuary, and some fine paintings by Karel Škréta and Petr Brandl. At press time the National Gallery's medieval Czech art collection was set to move from here to another monastery, the Klášter svaté Anežky České in the Old Town (☞ *above*), in November 2000. It's worth seeking out, for this fascinating trove contains some of the most memorable artworks made in northern Europe during the high- and late-Gothic periods, by influential Bohemian painters such as Master Theodoric and the Master of the Třeboň Altar. *Nám. U sv. Jiří, tel. 02/5732–0536. 90 Kč. Tues.–Sun. 10–6.*

50 **KRÁLOVSKÁ ZAHRADA** (Royal Garden). This peaceful swath of greenery affords an unusually lovely view of St. Vitus's Cathedral and the castle's walls and bastions. Originally laid out in the 16th century, it endured devastation in war, neglect in times of peace, and many redesigns, reaching its present parklike form early this century. Luckily, its Renaissance treasures survive. One of these is the long, narrow **Míčovna** (Ball Game Hall), built by

Bonifaz Wohlmut in 1568, its garden front completely covered by a dense tangle of allegorical sgraffiti.

The **Královský letohrádek** (Royal Summer Palace, also known as the Belvedere), at the garden's eastern end, deserves its usual description as one of the most beautiful Renaissance structures north of the Alps. Italian architects began it; Wohlmut finished it off in the 1560s with a copper roof like an upturned boat's keel riding above the graceful arcades of the ground floor. During the 18th and 19th centuries, military engineers tested artillery in the interior, which had already lost its rich furnishings to Swedish soldiers during their siege of the city in 1648. The Renaissance-style *giardinetto* (little garden) adjoining the summer palace centers on another masterwork, the Italian-designed, Czech-cast Singing Fountain, which resonates to the sound of falling water. *Garden entrances from U Prašného mostu ul. and Mariánské hradby ul. near Chotkovy Park. Free. Apr.–Oct., daily 10–5:45.*

54 KRÁLOVSKÝ PALÁC (Royal Palace). The palace is an accumulation of the styles and add-ons of many centuries. The best way to grasp its size is from within the **Vladislavský sál** (Vladislav Hall), the largest secular Gothic interior space in Central Europe. The enormous hall was completed in 1493 by Benedikt Ried, who was to late-Bohemian Gothic what Peter Parler was to the earlier version. The room imparts a sense of space and light, softened by the sensuous lines of the vaulted ceilings and brought to a dignified close by the simple oblong form of the early Renaissance windows. In its heyday, the hall was the site of jousting tournaments, festive markets, banquets, and coronations. In more recent times, it has been used to inaugurate presidents, from the Communist Klement Gottwald in 1948 to Václav Havel in 1989, 1993, and 1998.

From the front of the hall, turn right into the rooms of the **Česká kancelář** (Bohemian Chancellery). This wing was built by the same Benedikt Ried only 10 years after the hall was completed, but it shows a much stronger Renaissance influence. Pass through the Renaissance portal into the last chamber of the chancellery. This room was the site of the second defenestration of Prague, in 1618, an event that marked the beginning of the Bohemian rebellion and, ultimately, the Thirty Years' War. This peculiarly Bohemian method of expressing protest (throwing someone out a window) had first been used in 1419 in the New Town Hall, during the lead-up to the Hussite wars. Two hundred years later the same conflict was reexpressed in terms of Hapsburg-backed Catholics versus Bohemian Protestants. Rudolf II had reached an uneasy agreement with the Bohemian nobles, allowing them religious freedom in exchange for financial support. But his next-but-one successor, Ferdinand II, was a rabid opponent of Protestantism and disregarded Rudolf's tolerant "Letter of Majesty." Enraged, the Protestant nobles stormed the castle and chancellery and threw two Catholic officials and their secretary, for good measure, out the window. Legend has it they landed on a mound of horse dung and escaped unharmed, an event the Jesuits interpreted as a miracle. The square window in question is on the left as you enter the room.

At the back of the Vladislav Hall, a staircase leads up to a gallery of the **Kaple všech svatých** (All Saints' Chapel). Little remains of Peter Parler's original work, but the church contains some fine works of art. The large room to the left of the staircase is the **Stará sněmovna** (council chamber), where the Bohemian nobles met with the king in a kind of prototype parliament. The descent from Vladislav Hall toward what remains of the **Romanský palác** (Romanesque Palace) is by way of a wide, shallow set of steps. This **Jezdecké schody** (Riders' Staircase) was the entranceway for knights who came for the jousting tournaments. *Royal Palace, Třetí nádvoří. For admission information, see Informační středisko, above. Apr.–Oct., daily 9–5; Nov.–Mar., daily 9–4.*

⑤⑧ LOBKOVICKÝ PALÁC (Lobkowicz Palace). From the beginning of the 17th century until the 1940s, this building was the residence of the powerful Catholic Lobkowicz family. It was supposedly to this house that the two defenestrated officials escaped after landing on the dung hill in 1618. During the 1970s the building was restored to its early Baroque appearance and now houses the National Museum's permanent exhibition on Czech history. If you want to get a chronological understanding of Czech history from the beginnings of the Great Moravian Empire in the 9th century to the Czech national uprising in 1848, this is the place. Copies of the crown jewels are on display here, but it is the rich collection of illuminated Bibles, old musical instruments, coins, weapons, royal decrees, paintings, and statues that makes the museum well worth visiting. Detailed information on the exhibits is available in English. *Jiřská ul. 40 Kč. Tues.–Sun. 9–5.*

④⑧ MATYÁŠOVA BRÁNA (Matthias Gate). Built in 1614, the stone gate once stood alone in front of the moats and bridges that surrounded the castle. Under the Hapsburgs, the gate survived by being grafted as a relief onto the palace building. As you go through it, notice the ceremonial white-marble entrance halls on either side that lead up to President Václav Havel's reception rooms (which are only rarely open to the public).

④⑦ PRVNÍ NÁDVOŘÍ (First Courtyard). The main entrance to Prague Castle from Hradčanské náměstí is a little disappointing. Going through the wrought-iron gate, guarded at ground level by Czech soldiers and from above by the ferocious *Battling Titans* (a copy of Ignaz Platzer's original 18th-century work), you'll enter this courtyard, built on the site of old moats and gates that once separated the castle from the surrounding buildings and thus protected the vulnerable western flank. The courtyard is one of the more recent additions to the castle, designed by Maria Theresa's court architect, Nicolò Pacassi, in the 1760s. Today it forms part of the presidential office complex. Pacassi's reconstruction was intended to unify the eclectic collection of buildings that made up the castle, but the effect of his work is somewhat flat.

⑤₂ TŘETÍ NÁDVOŘÍ (Third Courtyard). The contrast between the cool, dark interior of St. Vitus's Cathedral (☞ *above*) and the brightly colored Pacassi facades of the Third Courtyard just outside is startling. The courtyard's clean lines are the work of Slovenian architect Jože Plečnik in the 1930s, but the modern look is a deception. Plečnik's paving was intended to cover an underground world of house foundations, streets, and walls dating from the 9th through 12th centuries and rediscovered when the cathedral was completed. (You can see a few archways through a grating in a wall of the cathedral.) Plečnik added a few eclectic features to catch the eye: a granite obelisk to commemorate the fallen of the First World War, a black-marble pedestal for the Gothic statue of St. George (a copy of the National Gallery's original statue), the inconspicuous entrance to his Bull Staircase leading down to the south garden, and the peculiar golden ball topping the eagle fountain near the eastern end of the courtyard.

⑤₇ ZLATÁ ULIČKA (Golden Lane). An enchanting collection of tiny, ancient, brightly colored houses crouches under the fortification wall, looking remarkably like a set for *Snow White and the Seven Dwarfs*. Legend has it that these were the lodgings of the international group of alchemists whom Rudolf II brought to the court to produce gold. The truth is a little less romantic: the houses were built during the 16th century for the castle guards, who supplemented their income by practicing various crafts outside the jurisdiction of the powerful guilds. By the early 20th century, Golden Lane had become the home of poor artists and writers. Franz Kafka, who lived at No. 22 in 1916 and 1917, described the house on first sight as "so small, so dirty, impossible to live in and lacking everything necessary." But he soon came to love the place. As he wrote to his fiancée: "Life here is something special . . . to close out the world not just by shutting the door to a room or apartment but to the whole house, to step out into the snow of the silent lane." The lane now houses tiny stores selling books, music, and crafts.

Within the walls above Golden Lane, there is a timber-roof ☞ **corridor** lined with replica suits of armor and weapons (some of it for sale), mock torture chambers, and the like. At the far end ☞ of the lane is the private **Muzeum hraček** (Toy Museum). The building once belonged to a high royal official called the Supreme Burgrave. *Corridor: enter between No. 23 and No. 24. Toy Museum: enter from Jiřská ul. Corridor free, Toy Museum 40 Kč. Corridor Tues.–Sun. 10–6, Mon. 1–6; Toy Museum daily 9:30–5:30.*

NOVÉ MĚSTO (NEW TOWN) AND VYŠEHRAD

To this day, Charles IV's building projects are tightly woven into the daily lives of Praguers. His most extensive scheme, the New Town, is still such a lively, vibrant area you may hardly realize that its streets, Gothic churches, and squares were planned as far back as 1348. With Prague fast outstripping its Old Town parameters, Charles IV extended the city's fortifications. A high wall surrounded the newly developed 2½ square km (1½ square mi) area south and east of the Old Town, tripling the walled territory on the Vltava's right bank. The wall extended south to link with the fortifications of the citadel called Vyšehrad. In the mid-19th century, new building in the New Town boomed in a welter of Romantic and neo-Renaissance styles, particularly on Wenceslas Square and avenues such as Vodičkova, Na Poříčí, and Spálená. One of the most important structures was the Národní divadlo (National Theater), meant to symbolize in stone the revival of the Czechs' history, language, and sense of national pride. Both preceding and following Czechoslovak independence in 1918, modernist architecture entered the mix, particularly on the outer fringes of the Old Town and in the New Town. One of modernism's most unexpected products was

Cubist architecture, a form unique to Prague, which produced four notable examples at the foot of ancient Vyšehrad.

A Good Walk

Václavské náměstí ③, marked by the **Statue of St. Wenceslas** ③, is a long, gently sloping boulevard rather than a square in the usual sense. It is bounded at the top (the southern end) by the **Národní muzeum** ③ and at the bottom by the pedestrian shopping areas of Národní třída and Na Příkopě. Today Václavské náměstí has Prague's liveliest street scene. Don't miss the dense maze of arcades tucked away from the street in buildings that line both sides. You'll find an odd assortment of cafés, shops, ice cream parlors, and movie houses, all seemingly unfazed by the passage of time. One eye-catching building on the square is the Hotel Europa, at No. 25, a riot of Art Nouveau that recalls the glamorous world of turn-of-the-20th-century Prague. Work by the Czech artist whose name is synonymous with Art Nouveau is on show just a block off the square, via Jindřišská, at the **Mucha Museum.**

From the foot of square, head down 28 října to Jungmannovo náměstí, a small square named for the linguist and patriot Josef Jungmann (1773–1847). In the courtyard off the square at No. 18, have a look at the Kostel Panny Marie Sněžné (Church of the Virgin Mary of the Snows). Building ceased during the Hussite wars, leaving a very high, foreshortened church that never grew into the monumental structure planned by Charles IV. Beyond it lies a quiet sanctuary: the walled Františkánská zahrada (Franciscan Gardens). A busy shopping street, Národní třída, extends from Jungmannovo náměstí about ¾ km (½ mi) to the river and the **Národní divadlo** ③. From the theater, follow the embankment, Masarykovo nábřeží, south toward Vyšehrad. Note the Art Nouveau architecture of No. 32, the amazingly eclectic design by Kamil Hilbert at No. 26, and the tile-decorated Hlahol building at No. 16. Opposite, on a narrow island, is a 19th century, yellow-and-white ballroom-restaurant, Žofín.

Straddling an arm of the river at Myslíkova ulice are the modern Galerie Mánes (1928–30) and its attendant 15th-century water tower, where, from a lookout on the sixth floor, Communist-era secret police used to observe Václav Havel's apartment at Rašínovo nábřeží 78. This building, still part-owned by the president, and the adjoining **Tančící dům** are on the far side of a square named Jiráskovo náměstí after the historical novelist Alois Jirásek. From this square, Resslova ulice leads uphill four blocks to a much larger, parklike square, **Karlovo náměstí** ⑩.

If you have the energy to continue on toward Vyšehrad, a convenient place to rejoin the riverfront is Palackého náměstí via Na Moráni street at the southern end of Karlovo náměstí. The square has a (melo)dramatic monument to the 19th-century historian František Palacký, "awakener of the nation," and the view from here of the Benedictine Klášter Emauzy is lovely. The houses grow less attractive south of here, so you may wish to hop a tram (No. 3, 16, or 17 at the stop on Rašínovo nábřeží) and ride one stop to Výtoň, at the base of the **Vyšehrad** ⑪ citadel. Walk under the railroad bridge on Rašínovo nábřeží to find the closest of four nearby **Cubist buildings.** Another lies just a minute's walk farther along the embankment; two more are on Neklanova, a couple of minutes' walk "inland" on Vnislavova. To get up to the fortress, make a hard left onto Vratislavova (the street right before Neklanova), an ancient road that runs tortuously up into the heart of Vyšehrad.

It's about 2¼ km (1½ mi) between Národní divadlo and Vyšehrad. Note that Tram No. 17 travels the length of the embankment, if you'd like to make a quicker trip between the two points.

TIMING

You might want to divide the walk into two parts, first taking in the busy New Town between Václavské náměstí and Karlovo náměstí, then doing Vyšehrad and the Cubist houses as a side trip. A leisurely stroll from the Národní divadlo to Vyšehrad may easily absorb two hours, as may an exploration of Karlovo náměstí and the Klášter Emauzy. Vyšehrad is open every day, year-round, and the views are stunning on a clear day or evening, but keep in mind that there is little shade along the river walk on hot afternoons.

Sights to See

CUBIST BUILDINGS. Born of zealous modernism, Prague's Cubist architecture followed a great Czech tradition in that it fully embraced new ideas while adapting them to existing artistic and social contexts. Between 1912 and 1914, Josef Chochol (1880–1956) designed several of the city's dozen or so Cubist projects. His apartment house **Neklanova 30**, on the corner of Neklanova and Přemyslova, is a masterpiece in dingy concrete. The pyramidal, kaleidoscopic window mouldings and roof cornices are completely novel while making an expressive link to Baroque forms; the faceted corner balcony column elegantly alludes to Gothic forerunners. On the same street, at **Neklanova 2**, is another apartment house attributed to Chochol; like the building at Neklanova 30, it uses pyramidal shapes and the suggestion of Gothic columns.

Chochol's **villa,** on the embankment at Libušina 3, has an undulating effect created by smoothly articulated forms. The wall and gate around the back of the house use triangular mouldings and metal grating to create an effect of controlled energy. The **three-family house,** about 100 yards away from the villa at Rašínovo nábřeží 6–10, was completed slightly earlier, when Chochol's Cubist style was still developing. Here, the design is touched with Baroque and neoclassical influence, with a mansard roof and end gables.

40 KARLOVO NÁMĚSTÍ (Charles Square). This square began life as a cattle market, a function chosen by Charles IV when he established the New Town in 1348. The horse market (now Wenceslas Square) quickly overtook it as a livestock-trading center, and an untidy collection of shacks accumulated here until the mid-1800s, when it became a green park named for its patron.

Novoměstská radnice (New Town Hall), at the northern edge of the square, has a late-Gothic tower similar to that of the Old Town Hall and three tall Renaissance gables. The first defenestration of Prague occurred here on July 30, 1419, when a mob of townspeople, followers of the martyred religious reformer Jan Hus, hurled Catholic town councillors out the windows. Historical exhibitions and contemporary art shows are held here regularly (admission prices vary), and you can climb the tower for a view of the New Town. *Karlovo nám. at Vodičkova, Prague 2. Tower 20 Kč. Tower June–Sept., Tues.–Sun. 10–6.*

Just south of the square lies another of Charles IV's gifts to the city, the Benedictine **Klášter Emauzy** (Emmaus Monastery). It is often called Na Slovanech, literally "At the Slavs'," in reference to its purpose when established in 1347: the emperor invited Croatian monks here to celebrate mass in Old Slavonic and thus cultivate religion among the Slavs in a city largely controlled by Germans. A faded but substantially complete cycle of biblical scenes by Charles's court artists lines the four cloister walls. The frescoes, and especially the abbey church, suffered heavy damage from a February 14, 1945, raid by Allied bombers that may have mistaken Prague for Dresden, 121 km (75 mi) away. The church lost its spires, and the interior remains a blackened shell. Some years after the war, two curving concrete "spires" were set atop the church. *Vyšehradská 49 (cloister entrance on the left at the rear of the church). 10 Kč. Weekdays 8–6 or earlier depending on daylight.*

MUCHA MUSEUM. For decades it was almost impossible to find an Alfons Mucha original in the homeland of this famous Czech artist, until, in 1998, this private museum opened with nearly 100 works from his long career. What you'd expect to see is here—the theater posters of actress Sarah Bernhardt; the magazine covers; the luscious, sinuous Art Nouveau designs—

and there are also paintings, photographs taken in Mucha's studio (one shows Paul Gauguin playing the piano in his underwear), and even Czechoslovak banknotes designed by the artist. *Panská 7 (1 block off Wenceslas Square, across from the Palace Hotel), tel. 02/628–4162. 120 Kč. Daily 10–6.*

39 NÁRODNÍ DIVADLO (National Theater). The idea for a Czech national theater began during the revolutionary decade of the 1840s. In a telling display of national pride, donations to fund the plan poured in from all over the country, from people of every socioeconomic stratum. The cornerstone was laid in 1868, and the "National Theater generation" who built the neo-Renaissance structure became the architectural and artistic establishment for decades to come. Its designer, Josef Zítek (1832–1909), was the leading neo-Renaissance architect in Bohemia. The nearly finished interior was gutted by a fire in 1881, and Zítek's onetime student Josef Schulz (1840–1917) saw the reconstruction through to completion two years later. Statues representing Drama and Opera rise above the riverfront side entrances; two gigantic chariots flank figures of Apollo and the nine Muses above the main facade. The performance space itself is filled with gilding, voluptuous plaster figures, and plush upholstery. Next door is the modern (1970s–80s) Nová scéna (New Stage), where the popular Magic Lantern black-light shows are staged. The Národní divadlo is one of the best places to see a performance; ticket prices start as low as 30 Kč. *Národní třída 2, tel. 02/2490–1448.*

38 NÁRODNÍ MUZEUM (National Museum). This imposing structure, designed by Prague architect Josef Schulz and built between 1885 and 1890, does not come into its own until it is bathed in nighttime lighting. By day the grandiose edifice seems an inappropriate venue for a musty collection of stones and bones, minerals, and coins. This museum is only for dedicated fans of the genre. *Václavské nám. 68, tel. 02/2449–7111. 70 Kč. May–Sept., daily 10–6; Oct.–Apr., daily 9–5; closed 1st Tues. of month.*

❸❼ STATUE OF ST. WENCESLAS. Josef Václav Myslbek's huge equestrian grouping of St. Wenceslas with other Czech patron saints around him is a traditional meeting place at times of great national peril or rejoicing. In 1939, Praguers gathered to oppose Hitler's takeover of Bohemia and Moravia. It was here also, in 1969, that the student Jan Palach set himself on fire to protest the bloody invasion of his country by the Soviet Union and other Warsaw Pact countries in August of the previous year. The invasion ended the "Prague Spring," a cultural and political movement emphasizing free expression, which was supported by Alexander Dubček, the popular leader at the time. Although Dubček never intended to dismantle Communist authority completely, his political and economic reforms proved too daring for fellow comrades in the rest of Eastern Europe. In the months following the invasion, conservatives loyal to the Soviet Union were installed in all influential positions. The subsequent two decades were a period of cultural stagnation. Hundreds of thousands of Czechs and Slovaks left the country, a few became dissidents, and many more resigned themselves to lives of minimal expectations and small pleasures. *Václavské náměstí.*

TANČÍCÍ DŮM (Dancing House). This whimsical building was partnered into life in 1996 by architect Frank Gehry (of Guggenheim Museum in Bilbao fame) and his Croatian-Czech collaborator Vlado Milunic. A wasp-waisted glass-and-steel tower sways into the main structure as though they were a couple on the dance floor—a "Fred and Ginger" effect that gave the wacky, yet somehow appropriate, building its nickname. A French restaurant occupies the top floors (☞ La Perle de Prague in Eating Out), and there is a café at street level. *Rašínovo nábř. 80.*

❸❻ VÁCLAVSKÉ NÁMĚSTÍ (Wenceslas Square). You may recognize this spot from your television set, for it was here that some 500,000 students and citizens gathered in the heady days of November 1989 to protest the policies of the former Communist regime. The government capitulated after a week of demonstrations, without a shot fired or the loss of a single life, bringing to power the first democratic government in 40 years (under playwright-president Václav Havel). Today this peaceful transfer of power is half-ironically referred to as the "Velvet" or "Gentle" Revolution (*něžná revoluce*). It was only fitting that the 1989 revolution should take place on Wenceslas Square: throughout much of Czech history, the square has served as the focal point for popular discontent. The long "square" was first laid out by Charles IV in 1348 as a horse market at the center of the New Town.

At No. 25, the **Hotel Europa** is an Art Nouveau gem, with elegant stained glass and mosaics in the café and restaurant. The terrace is an excellent spot for people-watching.

④ **VYŠEHRAD.** Bedřich Smetana's symphonic poem *Vyšehrad* opens with four bardic harp chords that seem to echo the legends surrounding this ancient fortress. Today, the flat-top bluff standing over the right bank of the Vltava is a green, tree-dotted expanse showing few signs that splendid medieval monuments once made it a landmark to rival Prague Castle. With its neo-Gothic spires, **Kapitulní kostel svatých Petra a Pavla** (Chapter Church of Sts. Peter and Paul) dominates the plateau as it has since the 11th century. Next to the church lies the burial ground of the nation's revered cultural figures. Most of the buildings still standing are from the 19th century, but scattered among them are a few older structures and some foundation stones of the medieval palaces. Surrounding the ruins are gargantuan, excellently preserved brick fortifications built from the 17th to the mid-19th century; their broad tops allow strollers to take in sweeping vistas up- and downriver.

The historical father of Vyšehrad, the "High Castle," is Vratislav II (ruled 1061–92), a Přemyslid duke who became first king of Bohemia. He made the fortified hilltop his capital, but, under subsequent rulers, it fell into disuse until the 14th century, when Charles IV transformed the site into an ensemble of palaces, the Gothicized main church, battlements, and a massive gatehouse called Špička, whose scant remains are on V pevnosti ulice. By the 17th century, royalty had long since departed, and most of the structures they built were crumbling. Vyšehrad was turned into a fortress.

Vyšehrad's place in the modern Czech imagination is largely thanks to the National Revivalists of the 19th century, particularly writer Alois Jirásek (1851–1930), who mined medieval chronicles for legends and facts to glorify the early Czechs. In his rendition, Vyšehrad was the court of the prophetess-ruler Libuše, who had a vision of her husband-to-be, the ploughman Přemysl—father of the Přemyslid line—and of "a city whose glory shall reach the heavens" called Praha. (In truth, the Czechs first came to Vyšehrad around the beginning of the 900s, slightly later than the building of Prague Castle.)

A concrete result of the National Revival was the establishment of the **Hřbitov** (cemetery) in the 1860s—it peopled the fortress with the remains of luminaries from the arts and sciences. The grave of Smetana faces the Slavín, a mausoleum for more than 50 honored men and women including Alfons Mucha, sculptor Jan Štursa, inventor František Křižík, and the opera diva Ema Destinnová. All are guarded by a winged genius who hovers above the inscription AČZEMŘELI, JEŠTĚMLUVÍ ("ALTHOUGH THEY HAVE DIED, THEY YET SPEAK"). ANTONÍN DVOŘÁK (1841–1904) rests in the arcade along the north wall of the cemetery. Among the many writers buried here are Jan Neruda, Božena Němcová, Karel Čapek, and the Romantic poet Karel Hynek Mácha, whose grave was visited by students on their momentous November 17, 1989, protest march.

Traces of the citadel's distant past do remain. A heavily restored **Romanesque rotunda,** built by Vratislav II, stands on the east side of the compound. Foundations and a few embossed floor tiles from the late-10th-century **Basilika svatého Vavřince** (St. Lawrence Basilica) are in a structure on Soběslavova street (if it is locked, you can ask for the key at the refreshment stand just to the left of the basilica entrance; admission is 5 Kč). Part of the medieval fortifications stand next to the surprisingly confined foundation mounds of a medieval palace overlooking a ruined watchtower called Libuše's Bath. A nearby plot of grass hosts a statue of Libuše and her consort Přemysl, one of four large sculpted images of couples from Czech legend by J. V. Myslbek (1848–1922), the sculptor of the St. Wenceslas monument.

The military history of the fortress and the city is covered in a small exposition inside the **Cihelná brána** (Brick Gate). The gate is also the entrance to the casemates—a long, dark passageway within the walls that ends at a dank hall used to store several original, pollution-scarred Charles Bridge sculptures. A guided tour into the casemates and the statue storage room starts at the military history exhibit. *Entrances on Vratislavova ul. and V pevnosti ul. Information center: V pevnosti. Casemates tour 20 Kč, military exhibit 10 Kč. Grounds daily. Casemates, military history exhibit, St. Lawrence Basilica Apr.–Oct., daily 9:30–5:30; Nov.–Mar., daily 9:30–4:30. Cemetery Apr.–Oct., daily 8–6; Nov.–Mar., daily 8–4. Metro: Vyšehrad.*

VINOHRADY

From Riegrovy Park and its sweeping view of the city from above the National Museum, the eclectic apartment houses and villas of the elegant residential neighborhood called Vinohrady extend eastward and southward. The pastel-tint ranks of turn-of-the-20th-century apartment houses—many crumbling after years of neglect—are slowly but unstoppably being transformed into upscale flats, slick offices, eternally packed new restaurants, and a range of shops unthinkable only a half decade ago. Much of the development lies on or near Vinohradská, the main street, which extends from the top of Wenceslas Square to a belt of enormous cemeteries about 3 km (2 mi) eastward. Yet the flavor of daily life persists: smoky old pubs still ply their trade on the quiet side streets; the stately theater, Divadlo na Vinohradech, keeps putting on excellent shows as it has for decades; and on the squares and in the parks nearly everyone still practices Prague's favorite form of outdoor exercise—walking the dog.

42 **KOSTEL NEJSVĚTĚJŠÍHO SRDCE PÁNĚ** (Church of the Most Sacred Heart). If you've had your fill of Romanesque, Gothic, and Baroque, take the metro to the Jiřího z Poděbrad station (Line A) for a look at a startling Art Deco edifice. Designed in 1927 by Slovenian architect Jože Plečnik (the same architect commissioned to update Prague Castle), the church resembles a luxury ocean liner more than a place of worship. The effect was conscious: during the 1920s and 1930s, the avant-garde imitated mammoth objects of modern technology. Plečnik used many modern elements on the inside. Notice the hanging speakers, seemingly designed to bring the word of God directly to the ears of each worshiper. You may be able to find someone at the back entrance of the church who will let you walk up the long ramp into the fascinating glass clock tower. *Nám. Jiřího z Poděbrad. Daily 10–5.*

43 **NOVÝ ŽIDOVSKÝ HŘBITOV** (New Jewish Cemetery). Tens of thousands of Czechs find eternal rest in Vinohrady's cemeteries. In this, the newest of the city's half-dozen Jewish burial grounds, you'll find the modest **tombstone of Franz Kafka,** which seems grossly inadequate to Kafka's stature but oddly in proportion to his own modest ambitions. The cemetery is usually open, although guards sometimes inexplicably seal off the grounds. Men may be required to wear a yarmulke (you can buy one here). Turn right at the main cemetery gate and follow the wall for about 100 yards. Kafka's thin, white tombstone lies at the front of section 21. City maps may label the cemetery Židovské hřbitovy. *Vinohradská at Jana Želivského. Free. June–Aug., Sun.–Thurs. 9–5, Fri. 9–1; Sept.–May, Sun.–Thurs. 9–4, Fri. 9–1. Metro: Vyšehrad.*

44 **PAVILON.** This gorgeous, turn-of-the-20th-century, neo-Renaissance, three-story market hall is one of the most attractive sites in Vinohrady. It used to be a major old-style market, a vast space filled with stalls selling all varieties of foodstuffs plus the requisite grimy pub. After being spiffed up several years ago, it mutated into an upscale shopping mall. Off the tourist track, Pavilon is a good place to watch Praguers—those who can afford its shops' gleaming designer pens and Italian shoes—ostentatiously drinking in *la dolce vita*, cell phones in hand. *Vinohradská 50, tel. 02/2209–7111. Mon.–Sat. 8:30 AM–9 PM, Sun. noon–6.*

NEED A BREAK? A symbol of this bucolic neighborhood's intellectual leanings, the literary café **Literární kavárna G + G** (Čerchovská 4, tel. 02/627–3332) serves coffees and light desserts in a well-lit and welcoming shop brimming with books, newspapers, and magazines (most in Czech). It's a block east of Riegrovy Park, or two blocks off Vinohradská via U Kanálky. Several nights a week, the café hosts readings as well as intimate concerts of folk, jazz, or Romany (Gypsy) music.

LETNÁ AND HOLEŠOVICE

From above the Vltava's left bank, the large, grassy plateau called Letná gives you one of the classic views of the Old Town and the many bridges crossing the river. (To get to Letná from the Old Town, take Pařížská street north, cross the Čechův Bridge, and climb the stairs.) Beer gardens, tennis, and Frisbee attract people of all ages, while amateur soccer players emulate the professionals of Prague's top team, Sparta, which plays in the stadium just across the road. A 10-minute walk from Letná, down into the residential neighborhood of Holešovice, brings you to a massive, gray-blue building whose cool exterior gives no hint of the treasures of Czech and French modern art that line its corridors. Just north along Dukelských hrdinů street is Stromovka—a royal hunting preserve turned gracious park.

Smart Sightseeings

Savvy travelers and others who take their sightseeing seriously have skills worth knowing about.

DON'T PLAN YOUR VISIT IN YOUR HOTEL ROOM Don't wait until you pull into town to decide how to spend your days. It's inevitable that there will be much more to see and do than you'll have time for: choose sights in advance.

ORGANIZE YOUR TOURING Note the places that most interest you on a map, and visit places that are near each other during the same morning or afternoon.

START THE DAY WELL EQUIPPED Leave your hotel in the morning with everything you need for the day—maps, medicines, extra film, your guidebook, rain gear, and another layer of clothing in case the weather turns cooler.

TOUR MUSEUMS EARLY If you're there when the doors open you'll have an intimate experience of the collection.

EASY DOES IT See museums in the mornings, when you're fresh, and visit sit-down attractions later on. Take breaks before you need them.

STRIKE UP A CONVERSATION Only curmudgeons don't respond to a smile and a polite request for information. Most people appreciate your interest in their home town. And your conversations may end up being your most vivid memories.

GET LOST When you do, you never know what you'll find—but you can count on it being memorable. Use your guidebook to help you get back on track. Build wandering-around time into every day.

QUIT BEFORE YOU'RE TIRED There's no point in seeing that one extra sight if you're too exhausted to enjoy it.

TAKE YOUR MOTHER'S ADVICE Go to the bathroom when you have the chance. You never know what lies ahead.

45 LETENSKÉ SADY (Letna Park). Come to this large, shady park for an unforgettable view of Prague's bridges. From the enormous cement pedestal at the center of the park, the largest statue of Stalin in Eastern Europe once beckoned to citizens on the Old Town Square far below. The statue was ripped down in the 1960s, when Stalinism was finally discredited. On sunny Sundays expatriates often meet up here to play ultimate Frisbee.

46 VELETRŽNÍ PALÁC (Trade Fair Palace). The National Gallery's **Sbírka moderního a soucasného umění** (Collection of Modern and Contemporary Art) has become a keystone in the city's visual-arts scene since its opening in 1995, despite unclear leadership. Touring the vast spaces of this 1920s Constructivist exposition hall and its comprehensive collection of 20th-century Czech art is the best way to see how Czechs surfed the forefront of the avant-garde wave until the cultural freeze following the Communist takeover in 1948, which threw the visual arts into gloom and introspection. (Most of the collections languished in storage for decades, either because some cultural commissar forbade their public display or because there was no exhibition space.) Also on display are works by Western European, mostly French, artists from Delacroix to the present. Especially noteworthy are the early Cubist paintings by Picasso and Braque. The 19th-century Czech art collection of the National Gallery was installed in the palace in the summer of 2000. Watch the papers and posters for information on traveling shows and temporary exhibits by young Czech artists. *Dukelských hrdinů 47, tel. 02/2430–1111. 90 Kč. Tues.–Sun. 10–6 (Thurs. until 9).*

In This Chapter

Updated by Ky Krauthamer

eating out

DINING CHOICES IN PRAGUE have increased greatly in the past decade as hundreds of new places have opened to meet the soaring demand from tourists and locals alike. These days, out-and-out rip-offs have almost disappeared, but before paying up at the end of a meal it's a good idea to take a close look at the added cover charge on your bill. Also keep an eye out for a large fee tacked on to a credit card bill. In pubs and neighborhood restaurants, ask if there is a *denní lístek* (daily menu) of cheaper and often fresher selections, but note that many places provide daily menus for the midday meal only. Special local dishes worth making a beeline for include *cibulačka* (onion soup), *kulajda* (potato soup with sour cream), *svíčková* (beef sirloin in cream sauce), and *ovocné knedlíky* (fruit dumplings, often listed under "meatless dishes").

The crush of visitors has placed tremendous strain on the more popular restaurants. The upshot: reservations are an excellent idea, especially for dinner during peak tourist periods. If you don't have reservations, try arriving a little before standard meal times: 11:30 AM for lunch or 5:30 PM for dinner.

For a cheaper and quicker alternative to the sit-down establishments listed below, try a light meal at one of the city's growing number of street stands or fast-food places. Look for stands offering *párky* (hot dogs) or the fattier *klobásy* (grilled sausages served with bread and mustard). For more exotic fare, try the very good vegetarian cooking at **Country Life** (Melantrichova 15, in the Old Town, tel. 02/2421–3366). Chic new cafés and bakeries spring up all the time. **Vzpomínky na Afriku** (Rybná at Jakubská, near the Kotva department store) has the widest selection of gourmet coffees in town, served at the single table or to go.

CATEGORY	PRICE*
$$$$	over $40
$$$	$20–$40
$$	$10–$20
$	under $10

*per person for a three-course meal, excluding wine and tip

STARÉ MĚSTO (OLD TOWN)

$$$$ BELLEVUE. The first choice for visiting dignitaries and businesspeople blessed with expense accounts, Bellevue has creative, freshly prepared cuisine, more nouvelle than Bohemian— and the elegant setting not far from Charles Bridge doesn't hurt. Look for the lamb carpaccio with fresh rosemary, garlic, and extra-virgin olive oil, or the wild berries marinated in port and cognac, served with vanilla-and-walnut ice cream. Window seats have stunning views of Prague Castle. The Sunday jazz brunch is a winner, too. *Smetanovo nábř. 18, tel. 02/2222–1449.* AE, MC, V.

$$$$ JEWEL OF INDIA. Although generally Asian cooking of any stripe is not Prague's forte, here is a sumptuous spot well worth seeking out for northern Indian tandooris and other moderately spiced specialties, including some delicious vegetarian dishes. *Pařížská 20, tel. 02/2481–1010.* AE, MC, V. Metro: Staroměstská.

$$$$ V ZÁTIŠÍ. White walls and casual grace accentuate the subtle
★ flavors of smoked salmon, plaice, beef Wellington, and other non-Czech specialties. Here, as at most of the city's better establishments, the wine list has expanded in recent years and now includes most of the great wine-producing regions, though good Moravian vintages are still kept on hand. In behavior unusual for the city, the benign waiters fairly fall over each other to serve

diners. *Liliová 1 at Betlémské nám., tel. 02/2222–2025. AE, MC, V. www.praguefinedining.cz*

$$$ BAROCK. Call it chic or call it pretentious, Barock exemplifies the revolution in Prague's dining and social life since those uncool Communists decamped. Thai and Japanese dishes predominate, and there are other Asian choices and international standards. Although eating isn't the main point here—being seen is—the fish dishes and sushi won't let you down. *Pařížská 24, tel. 02/232– 9221. AE, DC, MC, V.*

$$ CHEZ MARCEL. At this authentic French bistro on a quiet street, you can get a little taste of that *other* riverside capital. French owned and operated, Chez Marcel has a smallish but reliable menu listing pâtés, salads, rabbit and chicken, and some of the best steaks in Prague. The specials board usually has some tempting choices, such as salmon, beef daube, or foie gras. *Haštalská 12, tel. 02/231–5676. No credit cards.*

$ KAVÁRNA SLAVIA. This legendary hangout for the best and ★ brightest in Czech arts—from composer Bedřich Smetana and poet Jaroslav Seifert to then-dissident Václav Havel—reopened after being held hostage in absurd real-estate wrangles for most of the 1990s. Its Art Deco decor is a perfect backdrop for people watching, and the vistas (the river and Prague Castle on one side, the National Theater on the other) are a compelling reason to linger for hours over a coffee—although it's not the best brew in town. The Slavia is a café to its core, but you can also get a light meal, such as a small salad with Balkan cheese, an open-face sandwich, or breakfast in the form of scrambled eggs (don't even think about toast). And despite what the old-guard coat-check lady will tell you on your way in, it is not obligatory to check your coat with her. *Smetanovo nábř. 1012/2, tel. 02/2422–0957. AE, MC, V.*

$ LOTOS. Banana ragout with polenta and broccoli strudel are two favorites at what is undoubtedly the best of the city's scant

prague dining

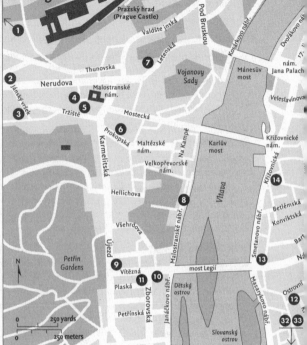

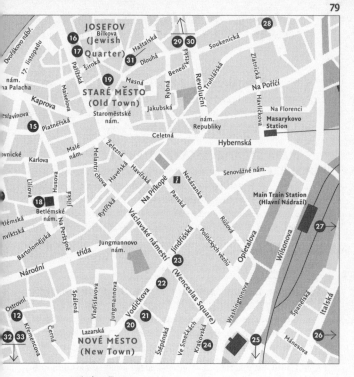

U Zlaté Hrušky, 1
Universal, 12
V Krakovské, 24
V Zátiší, 18

selection of all-vegetarian restaurants. Blond-wood tables and billowing tie-dye fabric set an informal yet elegant atmosphere. The salads and soups are wonderful. *Platnéřská 13, tel. 02/232–2390. MC, V.*

$ **PIZZERIA RUGANTINO.** Bright and spacious, this buzzing pizzeria serves up thin-crust pies; big, healthy salads; and good Italian bread. It can get quite loud when full, which is most nights. *Dušní 4, tel. 02/231–8172. No credit cards. No lunch Sun.*

MALÁ STRANA (LESSER QUARTER)

$$$$ **CIRCLE LINE.** Now moved out of the cellar into two elegant dining rooms, one done up in blue and the other in pink, Circle Line maintains its high standards with such dishes as fallow deer with spaetzle, pike perch, and yellowfin tuna carpaccio. The service can't be faulted. There are creative seasonal specials such as the warm foie gras with cherries, but be sure to save room for the chocolate plate for dessert. Brunch is served daily until 6 PM. *Malostranské nám. 12, tel. 02/5753–0022. AE, MC, V.*

$$$$ **PASHA.** This inviting Middle Eastern spot at the foot of Prague Castle hits just the right notes of luxury and easiness. The à la carte menu includes luscious *adana kebab* (skewer of minced lamb), pilaf, and shish kebab. Baklava served with fresh mint tea makes a splendid dessert. *Letenská 1, tel. 02/549–773. AE, MC, V. Closed Mon.*

$$$ **LOBKOVICKÁ.** This dignified *vinárna* (wine hall) set inside a 17th-
★ century town palace serves innovative, imaginative dishes by Prague standards. Chicken breast with crabmeat and curry sauce is an excellent main dish and typical of the kitchen's approach to sauces and spices. Deep red carpeting sets the perfect mood for enjoying bottles of Moravian wine. *Vlašská 17, tel. 02/530–185 or 02/5753–2511. AE, MC, V.*

$$$ **THE SUSHI BAR.** This chic little joint with the wacky whale sculpture floating overhead could have been transported straight from San Francisco. Given Prague's distance from the sea, the selection of

sushi and sashimi is excellent. For the same reason, call ahead to check when the fresh seafood is due (it's delivered twice a week), or stick to the broiled salmon or tempura dishes. *Zborovská 49, tel. 0603/244–882. DC, MC, V.*

\$\$\$ U MALTÉZSKÝCH RYTÍŘŮ. The tongue-twisting name means "At the Knights of Malta," a reference to the Catholic order whose embassy is nearby. The upstairs dining room and bar are cozy, but ask for a table in the deep cellar—then ask the proprietress to regale you with yarns about this ancient house. They've dropped some old favorites from the menu, but still offer good steaks, game, and fish. *Prokopská 10, tel. 02/5753–3666. AE, MC, V.*

\$\$\$ U MECENÁŠE. A fetching Renaissance inn from the 17th century, with dark, high-back benches in the front room and cozy, elegant sofas and chairs in back, this is a place to splurge. From the aperitifs to the specialty steaks or beef Wellington and the cognac (swirled lovingly in oversize glasses), the presentation is seamless. *Malostranské nám. 10, tel. 02/5753–1631. AE, MC, V.*

\$\$ RYBÁŘSKÝ KLUB. The "Fishing Club" restaurant shares its building
★ with a real fishing club's headquarters, and it's a great place to try a wide variety of freshwater fish. The friendly staff serves perch, eel, barbel, and the esteemed pike perch at picnic-style tables or by the water in summer. *U Sovových mlýnů 1, Kampa Island, tel. 02/ 530–223. MC, V.*

\$ BOHEMIA BAGEL. It's not New York, but the friendly, North American–owned Bohemia Bagel still serves up a plentiful assortment of fresh bagels, from raisin-walnut to "supreme," with all kinds of toppings. Their thick soups are among the best in Prague for the price, and the bottomless cups of coffee are a further draw. *Újezd 16, tel. 02/531–002. No credit cards.*

\$ CAFÉ SAVOY. Opened in 1887 as a grand café, the Savoy lasted only a few years before the long, airy room was divided up to be made into shops. In 1992 the café was reborn, and best of all, the painted and stuccoed ceiling that had long been covered over was restored. It's best for coffee, a drink, or a fine apple strudel; typical meat dishes such as pork steak with horseradish are also available. *Vítězná 5, no phone. AE, DC, MC, V.*

HRADČANY

$$$$ U ZLATÉ HRUŠKY. At this fetching little rococo house perched on one of Prague's prettiest cobblestone streets, slide into one of the cozy dark-wood booths and let the cheerful staff advise on wines and specials. Among the regular offerings are a superb leg of venison with pears and millet gnocchi and an excellent appetizer of duck liver in wine sauce. After dinner, stroll to the castle for an unforgettable panorama. *Nový Svět 3, tel. 02/2051–4778. AE, MC, V.*

$$ U ŠEVCE MATOUŠE. Steaks are the raison d'être at this former shoemaker's shop, where a gold shoe still hangs from the ceiling of the arcade outside to guide patrons into the vaulted dining room. Appetizers are hit-and-miss; stick with the dozen or so tenderloins and filet mignons. *Loretánské nám. 4, tel. 02/2051–4536. MC, V.*

NOVÉ MĚSTO (NEW TOWN) AND VYŠEHRAD

$$$$ LA PERLE DE PRAGUE. Delicious Parisian cooking awaits at the top of the curvaceous "Fred and Ginger" building. The interior of the main room is washed with soft tones of lilac and sea green. This room also has smallish windows—typical of architect Frank Gehry's designs—and rather cheesy nude photographs, but the semiprivate dining room at the very top has a riveting view over the river. Try the red snapper Provençal, freshwater *candát* (pike perch), or tournedos of beef Béarnaise. Make reservations as early as you can. This is also a good reason to unpack your tie. *Rašínovo nábř. 80, tel. 02/2198–4160. AE, DC, MC, V. Closed Sun. No lunch Mon.*

$$$ FAKHRELDINE. This elegant Lebanese restaurant, now at a more central location, offers an excellent range of authentic dishes, such as *kibbey bisayniyeh* (lamb and ground pine-nut patty), *warakinab* (stuffed grape leaves), and three kinds of baklava. For a moderately priced meal, try several *meze* (appetizers)—hummus and garlic yogurt, perhaps—instead of a main course. *Štěpánská 32, tel. 02/ 2223–2617. AE, DC, MC, V. Closed Sun.*

$$ BELLA NAPOLI. The decor may be a little much, but the food is
★ genuine and the price-to-quality ratio hard to beat. Close your eyes to the alabaster Venus de Milos astride shopping-mall fountains and head straight for the antipasto bar, which will distract you with fresh olives, eggplant, squid, and mozzarella. For your main course, go with any of a dozen superb pasta dishes or splurge with shrimp or chicken parmigiana. *V Jámě 8, tel. 02/ 2223–2933. No credit cards.*

$$ DOLLY BELL. This restaurant's whimsical design, with upside-down tables hanging from the ceiling, provides a clever counterpoint to the extensive selection of well-prepared Yugoslav dishes. There's an emphasis on meat and seafood—try the corn bread (polenta) with Balkan cheese, *čevapčiči* (pork sausage), and *tufahija* (baked apple with a smooth nut filling). *Neklanova 20, tel. 02/ 298–815. DC, MC, V.*

$$ FROMIN. Come dressed to the teeth—flourishing your mobile phone, preferably—for dinner at this cavernous, postmodern loft high above Wenceslas Square. The food is better than average, with entrées unusual for hereabouts, such as turkey steak with rosemary, lamb cutlets, and fresh tuna steaks. The upstairs café is quiet in the mornings; at 10 PM it becomes a disco whose doorman will turn away unstylishly dressed guests. *Václavské nám. 21, tel. 02/2423–2319. AE, MC, V.*

$ NOVOMĚSTSKÝ PIVOVAR. It's easy to lose your way in this crowded microbrewery-restaurant with its maze of rooms, some painted in mock-medieval style, others covered with murals of

Prague street scenes. *Vepřové koleno* (pork knuckle) is a favorite dish. The beer is the cloudy, fruity "fermented" style. *Vodičkova 20, tel. 02/2223–1662.* AE, MC, V.

$ PIZZERIA COLOSEUM. An early entry in the burgeoning pizza-and-pasta trade, this one has kept its popularity due largely to its position right off Wenceslas Square. Location doesn't have everything to do with it, though; the pizzas have a wonderfully thin, crisp crust, and the pasta with Gorgonzola sauce will have you blessing Italian cows. Long picnic tables make this an ideal spot for an informal lunch or dinner. There's a salad bar, too. *Vodičkova 32, tel. 02/2421–4914.* AE, MC, V.

$ RADOST FX CAFÉ. Colorful and campy in design, this lively café is a street-level adjunct to the popular Radost dance club. It's a vegetarian heaven for both Czechs and expatriates: the creative specials of a Mexican or Italian persuasion are tasty, and filling enough to satisfy carnivores. If you suddenly find yourself craving a brownie, this is the place to get a fudge fix. Another plus: it's open until around 3 AM. *Bělehradská 120, tel. 02/2425–4776. No credit cards.*

$ UNIVERSAL. A pioneer in the neighborhood behind the National Theater that's fast becoming a trendy dining ghetto, Universal serves up satisfying French- and Indian-influenced main courses, giant side orders of scalloped potatoes, and luscious lemon tarts or chocolate mousse—all at ridiculously low prices. *V Jirchářích 6, tel. 02/2491–8182. No credit cards.*

$ V KRAKOVSKÉ. At this clean, proper pub close to the major tourist sights, the food is traditional and hearty. This is the place to try *svíčková na smetaně* (thinly sliced sirloin beef in cream sauce) paired with an effervescent pilsner beer. *Krakovská 20, tel. 02/ 2221–0204. No credit cards.*

VINOHRADY

$$ MYSLIVNA. The name means "Hunting Lodge," and the cooks at this neighborhood eatery certainly know their way around venison, quail, and boar. Attentive staff can advise on wines: try Vavřinecké, a hearty red that holds its own with any beast. The stuffed quail and the leg of venison with walnuts get high marks. A cab from the city center to Myslivna should cost under 200 Kč. *Jagellonská 21, tel. 02/627–0209. AE, MC, V.*

LETNÁ AND HOLEŠOVICE

$ LA CRÊPERIE. Run by a Czech-French couple, this creperie near the Veletržní palác (Trade Fair Palace) serves all manner of crepes, both sweet and savory. (It may take at least three or four to satisfy a hearty appetite.) Make sure to leave room for the dessert crepe with cinnamon-apple purée layered with lemon cream. The wine list offers both French and Hungarian vintages. *Janovského 4, Holešovice, tel. 02/878–040. No credit cards.*

$ U POČTŮ. This is a charmingly old-fashioned neighborhood eatery with comparatively skilled service. Garlic soup and chicken livers in wine sauce are flawlessly rendered, and the grilled trout is delicious. *Milady Horákové 47, Letná, tel. 02/3337–1419. AE, MC, V.*

ŽIŽKOV

$ MAILSI. Funky paintings of Arabian Nights–type scenes in a low-
★ ceiling cellar make for a casual, cheerful setting at this Pakistani restaurant. Chicken is done especially well here—the *murgh vindaloo* may well be the spiciest dish in Prague, and the thin-sliced marinated chicken (*murgh tikka*) appetizer is a favorite. Take Tram 5, 9, or 26 to the Lipanská stop, then walk one block uphill. *Lipanská 1, tel. 02/9005–9706 or 0603/466–626. No credit cards.*

In This Chapter

Updated by Ky Krauthamer

shopping

DESPITE THE RELATIVE SHORTAGE of quality clothes—Prague has a long way to go before it can match shopping meccas Paris and Rome—the capital is a great place to pick up gifts and souvenirs. Bohemian crystal and porcelain deservedly enjoy a worldwide reputation for quality, and plenty of shops offer excellent bargains. The local market for antiques and art is still relatively undeveloped, although dozens of antiquarian bookstores harbor some excellent finds, particularly German and Czech books and graphics.

SHOPPING DISTRICTS

The major shopping areas are **Na Příkopě,** which runs from the foot of Wenceslas Square to náměstí Republiky (Republic Square), and the area around **Old Town Square.** The Old Town streets **Pařížská ulice** and **Karlova ulice** are dotted with boutiques and antiques shops. In the Lesser Quarter, try **Nerudova ulice,** the street that runs up to Hradčany.

DEPARTMENT STORES

Prague's department stores are not always well stocked and often have everything except the one item you're looking for, but a stroll through one may yield some interesting finds and bargains. **Bílá Labut'** (Na Poříčí 23, tel. 02/2481–1364) has a decent selection, but the overall shabbiness harkens back to socialist times. **Kotva** (Nám. Republiky 8, tel. 02/2480–1111) is comparatively upscale, with a nice stationery shop and a basement supermarket with wine and cheese aisles.

The centrally located **Tesco** (Národní třída 26, tel. 02/2200–3111) is generally the best place for one-stop shopping. It has same-day film developing, a newsstand that stocks English-language newspapers and magazines, American-brand toiletries, a supermarket with Western groceries (if you're dying for corn chips, you'll find them here), and a multilingual staff.

STREET MARKETS

For fruits and vegetables, the best street market in central Prague is on **Havelská ulice** in the Old Town. You'll need to arrive early in the day if you want something a bit more exotic than tomatoes and cucumbers. The biggest market for nonfood items is the flea market in **Holešovice,** north of the city center, although there isn't really much of interest here outside of cheap tobacco and electronics products. Take the metro (Line C) to the Vltavská station and then catch any tram heading east (running to the left as you exit the metro station). Exit at the first stop and follow the crowds.

SPECIALTY STORES
Antiques

For antiques connoisseurs, Prague can be a bit of a letdown. Even in comparison with other former Communist capitals such as Budapest, the choice of antiques in Prague can seem depressingly slim, as the city lacks large stores with a diverse selection of goods. The typical Prague *starožitnosti* (antiques shop) tends to be a small, one-room jumble of old glass and bric-a-brac. The good ones distinguish themselves by focusing on one particular specialty.

On the pricey end of the scale is the Prague affiliate of the Austrian **Dorotheum** auction house (Ovocný trh 2, tel. 02/2422–2001) in the Old Town. It is an elegant pawnshop that specializes in small things: jewelry, porcelain knickknacks, and standing clocks, as well as the odd military sword. The small **JHB**

Starožitnosti (Panská 1, tel. 02/261–425) in the New Town is the place for old clocks: everything from rococo to Empire standing clocks and Bavarian cuckoo clocks. The shop also has a wide array of antique pocket watches. **Nostalgie Antique** (Jánský Vršek 8, tel. 02/5753–0049) specializes in old textiles and jewelry. Most of the textiles are pre–World War II and include clothing, table linens, curtains, hats, and laces.

Papillio (Týn 1, tel. 02/2489–5454), in the elaborately refurbished medieval courtyard behind the Church of the Virgin Mary Before Týn, is probably one of the best antiques shops in Prague, offering furniture, paintings, and especially museum-quality antique glass. Here you can find colorful Biedermeier goblets by Moser and wonderful Loetz vases. **Zlatnictví Vomáčka** (Náprstkova 9, tel. 02/2222–2017) is a cluttered shop that redeems itself with its selection of old jewelry in a broad price range, including rare Art Nouveau rings and antique garnet brooches. In the shop's affiliate next door, jewelry is repaired, cleaned, and made to order.

Art Galleries

The best galleries in Prague are quirky and eclectic affairs, places to sift through artworks rather than browse at arms' length. Many galleries are also slightly off the beaten track and away from the main tourist thoroughfares. Prague's as-yet-untouristed Nový Svět neighborhood is something of a miniature artist's quarter and home to two of Prague's more interesting galleries. One is **Galerie Gambra** (Černínska 5, tel. 02/2051–4527), owned by the surrealist animator Jan Švankmajer. The space was originally Švankmajer's kitchen, where dissident surrealists used to gather and trade ideas; now the gallery displays Švankmajer's bizarre collages as well as his wife's anthropomorphic ceramics. Books and magazines focusing on Czech surrealist art are also for sale.

Galerie Nový Svět (Nový Svět 5, tel. 02/2051–4611) displays interesting paintings and drawings by somewhat obscure Czech artists, as well as ceramics, glass, and art books. At the higher end is **Galerie Peithner-Lichtenfels** (Michalská 12, tel. 02/2422–7680) in the Old Town, which specializes in modern Czech art. Paintings, prints, and drawings crowd the walls and are propped against glass cases and window sills. Comb through works by Czech Cubists, currently fetching high prices at international auctions.

Galerie Litera (Karlinske nám. 13, Prague 8, tel. 02/231–7195) is in Karlín, a neighborhood rarely set foot in by tourists—it's not rough but pretty seedy. (It's northeast of the city center; get off the metro at Florenc and walk five minutes up Sokolovská.) Most of the gallery space is given over to temporary shows of unique, high-quality graphics. There are also some lovely ceramics as well as a refined selection of antiquarian art books.

Books and Prints

Like its antiques shops, Prague's rare book shops, or *antikvariáts*, were once part of a massive state-owned consortium that, since privatization, has split up and diversified. Now most shops tend to cultivate their own specialties. Some have a small English-language section with a motley blend of potboilers, academic texts, classics, and tattered paperbacks. Books in German, on the other hand, are abundant.

Antikvariát Karel Křenek (Celetná 31, tel. 02/231–4734), near the Prašná brána (Powder Tower) in the Old Town, specializes in books with a humanist slant. It has a good selection of modern graphics and prides itself on its avant-garde periodicals and journals from the 1920s and 1930s. It also has a small collection of English books.

Antikvariát Makovský & Gregor (Kaprova 9, tel. 02/232–8335) is a great all-around bookstore as attested by the constant traffic of liberal-arts students from nearby Charles University. It's particularly fun to hunt around in the art section, where you could turn up the *Memoirs of Casanova* with illustrations by Aubrey Beardsley or a book on Leni Riefenstahl's mountaineering movies. If you'd just like a good read, be sure to check out the **Globe Bookstore and Coffeehouse** (Pšstrossova 6, tel. 02/2491–7230), a longtime magnet for the local English-speaking community, in its new, more central site.

U Karlova Mostu (Karlova 2, tel. 02/2222–0286) is the preeminent Prague bookstore. In a suitably bookish location opposite the Klementinum, it's the place to go if you are looking for that elusive 15th-century manuscript. In addition to housing ancient books too precious to be leafed through, the store has a good selection of books on local subjects, a small foreign-language section, and a host of prints, maps, drawings, and paintings. For new books in English, try **Anagram Books** (Týn 4, tel. 02/2489–5737). There's also a great selection around the corner at **Big Ben Bookshop** (Malá Štupartská 5, tel. 02/2482–6565).

Food and Wine

Specialty food and beverage stores are slowly catching on in Prague. **Fruits de France** (Jindřišská 9 and Bělehradská 94, tel. 02/9000–0339) charges Western prices for Prague's freshest fruits and vegetables, imported directly from France. **Cellarius** (Lucerna Passage [Wenceslas Square between Vodičkova and Štěpánská streets], tel. 02/2421–0979) has a wide choice of Moravian and Bohemian wines and spirits, as well as products from more recognized wine-making lands.

Fun Things for Children

Nearly every stationery store has beautiful watercolor and colored-chalk sets available at rock-bottom prices. The Czechs are also master illustrators, and the books they've made for young "pre-readers" are some of the world's loveliest. For delightful Czech-made wooden toys and wind-up trains, cars, and animals, look in at **Hračky** (Pohořelec 24, tel. 0604/757–214). For the child with a theatrical bent, a marionette—they range from finger-size to nearly child-size—can be a wonder (☞ Marionettes, *below*). For older children and teens, it's worth considering a Czech or Eastern European watch, telescope, or set of binoculars. The quality–price ratio is unbeatable.

Glass

Glass has traditionally been Bohemia's biggest export, and it was one of the few products manufactured during Communist times that managed to retain an artistically innovative spirit. Today Prague has plenty of shops selling Bohemian glass, much of it tourist kitsch. A good spot is the stylish **Galerie A** (Na Perštýně 10, tel. 02/261–334), which stocks Art Nouveau, Biedermeier, and medieval replica glass in Art Deco vitrines from the 1920s. Much more contemporary and decidedly less practical are the art-glass offerings at **Galerie 'Z'** (U lužického semináře 7, tel. 02/9005–5188), which sells limited-edition mold-melted and blown glass, and its sister shop, **Galerie Mozart** (Uhelný trh 11, tel. 02/2421–1127), off Národní třída, which also has glass sculptures and some colorful vases and bowls.

Moser (Na Příkopě 12, tel. 02/2421–1293), the opulent flagship store of the world-famous Karlovy Vary glassmaker, offers the widest selection of traditional glass. Even if you're not in the market to buy, stop by the store simply to look at the elegant wood-paneled salesrooms on the second floor. The staff will gladly pack goods for traveling.

Home Design

Czech design is wonderfully rich both in quality and imagination, emphasizing old-fashioned craftsmanship while often taking an offbeat, even humorous approach. Strained relations between Czech designers and producers have reined in the potential selection, but there are nevertheless a handful of places showcasing Czech work. **Fast** (Sázavská 32, Vinohrady, tel. 02/2425–0538) is a little bit off the beaten track but worth the trek. Besides ultramodern furniture, there are ingenious (and more portable) pens, binders, and other office and home accoutrements.

Arzenal (Valentinská 11, tel. 02/2481–4099) is a design shop that offers Japanese and Thai food in addition to vases and chairs; it exclusively sells work by Bořek Šípek, President Havel's official designer. **Galerie Bydlení** (Truhlářská 20, tel. 02/231–7743) is a father-and-son operation focusing exclusively on Czech-made furniture.

Jewelry

Alfons Mucha is perhaps most famous for his whiplash Art Nouveau posters, but he also designed furniture, lamps, clothing, and jewelry. **Art Décoratif** (U Obecního domu, tel. 02/2200–2350), right next door to the Art Nouveau Obecní D®m, sells Mucha-inspired designs—the jewelry is especially remarkable.

The Old Town's **Granát** (Dlouhá 30, tel. 02/231–5612) has a comprehensive selection of garnet jewelry, plus contemporary and traditional pieces set in gold and silver. **Halada** (Karlova 25, tel. 02/2421–8643) offers sleek, Czech-designed silver jewelry; an affiliate shop at Na Příkopě16 specializes in gold, diamonds, and pearls.

Marionettes

Marionettes have a long tradition in Bohemia, going back to the times when traveling troupes used to entertain children with morality plays on town squares. Now, although the art form survives, it has become yet another tourist lure, and you'll continually stumble across stalls selling almost identical marionettes. The marionettes at **Manhartský Dùm** (Celetná 17,

Beyond T-Shirts and Key Chains

You can't go wrong with baseball caps, refrigerator magnets, beer mugs, sweatshirts, T-shirts, key chains, and other local logo merchandise. You won't go broke buying these items, either.

BUDGET FOR A MAJOR PURCHASE If souvenirs are all about keeping the memories alive in the long haul, plan ahead to shop for something really special—a work of art, a rug or something else hand-crafted, or a major accessory for your home. One major purchase will stay with you far longer than a dozen tourist trinkets, and you'll have all the wonderful memories associated with shopping for it besides.

ADD TO YOUR COLLECTION Whether antiques, used books, salt and pepper shakers, or ceramic frogs are your thing, start looking in the first day or two. Chances are you'll want to scout around and then go back to some of the first shops you visited before you hand over your credit card.

GET GUARANTEES IN WRITING Is the vendor making promises? Ask him to put them in writing.

ANTICIPATE A SHOPPING SPREE If you think you might buy breakables, include a length of bubble wrap. Pack a large tote bag in your suitcase in case you need extra space. Don't fill your suitcase to bursting before you leave home. Or include some old clothing that you can leave behind to make room for new acquisitions.

KNOW BEFORE YOU GO Study prices at home on items you might consider buying while you're away. Otherwise you won't recognize a bargain when you see one.

PLASTIC, PLEASE Especially if your purchase is pricey and you're looking for authenticity, it's always smart to pay with a credit card. If a problem arises later on and the merchant can't or won't resolve it, the credit-card company may help you out.

tel. 02/2480–9156) are the real thing. These puppets—knights, princesses, and cloven-hoofed devils—are made by the same artists who supply professional puppeteers. Prices may be higher than for the usual stuff on the street, but the craftsmanship is well worth it.

Secondhand and antique marionettes are surprisingly hard to find. One place to look is **Antikva Ing. Bürger** (Betlémské nám. 8, in the courtyard, tel. 02/269–9148).

Musical Instruments

Hudební nástroje Kliment (Jungmannova nám. 17, tel. 02/2421–3966) carries a complete range of quality musical instruments at reasonable prices. **Capriccio** (Újezd 15, tel. 02/532–507) has sheet music of all kinds.

Sports Equipment

Kotva (☞ Department Stores, *above*) has a good selection of sports gear and clothing. For quality hiking and camping equipment, try **Hudy Sport** (Na Perštýně 14, tel. 02/2421–8600).

In This Chapter

Updated by Ky Krauthamer

outdoor activities and sports

PRAGUE PLAYS HOST to a variety of spectator sports, including world-class hockey, soccer, and tennis. There's room for growth in the participatory sports options for tourists, though the city makes a picturesque backdrop for any outdoor activity, from boating to golf to jogging.

PARTICIPANT SPORTS

Boats

Rowboats and paddle boats can be rented on Slovanský ostrov, the island in the Vltava just south of the National Theater.

Fitness Clubs

Some luxury hotels have well-equipped fitness centers with swimming pools. The **Corinthia Towers** (Kongresova 1, Prague 4, tel. 02/6119–1111) is south of the center, near the Vyšehrad metro station. The more centrally located **Hilton** (Pobřežní 1, Prague 8, tel. 02/2484–1111, Metro: Florenc) has full fitness facilities and tennis courts. Excellent and much less costly facilities can be found at the **Hotel Axa** (Na Poříčí 40, tel. 02/2481–2580).

Golf

Prague's only course is a nine-holer located in the western suburbs at the **Hotel Golf** (Plzeňská 215, tel. 02/5721–5185).

Take a taxi to the hotel or Tram 4, 7, or 9 from metro station Anděl to the Hotel Golf stop. **Praha Karlštejn Golf Club** offers a more challenging course with a view of the famous Karlštejn Castle. It's 30 km (18 mi) southwest of Prague, just across the Berounka River from the castle.

Jogging

The best place for jogging is **Stromovka,** a large, flat park adjacent to the Výstaviště fairgrounds in Prague 7 (take Tram 5, 12, or 17 to the Výstaviště stop). Closer to the center, another popular park is **Letenské sady** (Letna Park), the park east of the Royal Garden at Prague Castle, across Chotkova street (☞ Letná and Holešovice in Here and There). For safety's sake, unaccompanied women should avoid the more remote corners of this park.

SPECTATOR SPORTS

The best place to find out what's going on (and where) is the weekly sports page of the *Prague Post*, or you can inquire at your hotel.

Soccer

National and international matches are played regularly at the home of Prague's Sparta team, Sparta Stadium in Letná, behind Letna Park. To reach the stadium, take Tram 1, 25, or 26 to the Sparta stop.

Swimming

The best public swimming pool in Prague is at the **Podolí Swimming Stadium** in Podolí, which you can get to from the city center in 15 minutes or less by taking Tram 3 or 17 to the Kublov stop. The indoor pool is 50 meters long, and the complex also includes two open-air pools, a sauna, a steam bath, and a wild-ride water slide. (A word of warning: Podolí, for all its attractions, is notorious as a local hot spot of petty thievery.

Don't entrust any valuables to the lockers—it's best either to check them in the safe with the *vrátnice* [superintendent], or better yet, don't bring them at all.) The pools at the **Hilton** and **Hotel Axa** (☞ Fitness Clubs, *above*) are smaller but more conveniently located.

Tennis

There are public tennis courts at the **Strahov Stadium** in Břevnov. Take Bus 176 from Karlovo náměstí in the New Town, or Bus 143 from the Dejvická metro station (Line A), to the Stadium Strahov stop. The **Hilton** (☞ Fitness Clubs, *above*) has two public indoor courts.

In This Chapter

Updated by Ky Krauthamer

nightlife and the arts

THE FRATERNAL TWINS of the performing arts and nightlife continue to enjoy an exhilarating growth spurt in Prague, and the number of concerts, plays, musicals, and clubs keeps rising. Some venues in the city center pitch themselves to tourists, but there are dozens of places where you can join the local crowds for music, dancing, or the rituals of beer and conversation. For details of cultural and nightlife events, look for the English-language newspaper the *Prague Post* or one of the multilingual monthly guides available at hotels, tourist offices, and newsstands.

NIGHTLIFE
Cabaret

For adult stage entertainment (with some nudity) try the **Varieté Praga** (Vodičkova 30, tel. 02/2421–5945).

Discos

Dance clubs come and go regularly. The longtime favorite is **Radost FX** (Bělehradská 120, tel. 02/2251–3144), with imported and homegrown DJs playing the latest house, hip-hop, and dance music. **Karlovy Lázně** (Novotného lávka), near the Charles Bridge, is a four-story dance palace with everything from Czech oldies to ambient chill-out sounds. **La Habana** (Míšeňská 12, tel. 02/5731–5104), is the place to show off your moves to recorded salsa and merengue music.

Jazz Clubs

Jazz gained notoriety under the Communists as a subtle form of protest, and the city still has some great jazz clubs, featuring everything from swing to blues and modern. The listed clubs have a cover charge. **Reduta** (Národní 20, tel. 02/2491–2246) features a full program of local and international musicians. **AghaRTA** (Krakovská 5, tel. 02/2221–1275) offers a variety of jazz acts in an intimate space. Music starts around 9 PM, but come earlier to get a seat.

Jazz Club Železná (Železná 16, tel. 02/2421–2541) mixes its jazz acts with world music. **Jazz Club U staré paní** (Michalská 9, tel. 02/264–920) has a rotating list of tried-and-true Czech bands.

Pubs, Bars, and Lounges

Bars and lounges are not traditional Prague fixtures, but bars catering to a young crowd have elbowed their way in over the past few years. Still, most social life of the drinking variety takes place in pubs (*pivnice* or *hospody*), which are liberally sprinkled throughout the city's neighborhoods. Tourists are welcome to join in the evening ritual of sitting around large tables and talking, smoking, and drinking beer. Before venturing in, however, it's best to familiarize yourself with a few points of pub etiquette: Always ask if a chair is free before sitting down (*Je tu volno?*). To order a beer (*pivo*), do not wave the waiter down or shout across the room; he will usually assume you want beer—most pubs serve one brand—and bring it over to you without asking. He will also bring subsequent rounds to the table without asking. To refuse, just shake your head or say no thanks (*ne, děkuju*). At the end of the evening, usually around 10:30 or 11, the waiter will come to tally the bill.

There are plenty of popular pubs in the city center, all of which can get impossibly crowded. **U Medvídků** (Na Perštýně 7, tel. 02/2421–1916) was a brewery at least as long ago as the 15th century. Beer is no longer made on the premises; rather, they serve draft Budvar shipped from České Budějovice. **U svatého Tomáše** (Letenská 12, tel. 02/5732–0101) brewed beer for Augustinian monks starting in 1358. Now they serve commercially produced beer in a tourist-friendly mock-medieval hall in the Lesser Quarter. **U Zlatého Tygra** (Husova 17, tel. 02/2222–1111) is famed as one of the three best Prague pubs for Pilsner Urquell, the original and perhaps the greatest of the pilsners. It also used to be a hangout for such raffish types as the writer Bohumil Hrabal, who died in 1997.

One of the oddest phenomena of Prague's post-1989 renaissance is the sight of travelers and tour groups from the United States, Britain, Australia, and even Japan descending on this city to experience the life of—American expatriates. There are a handful of bars guaranteed to ooze Yanks and other native English speakers. The **James Joyce Pub** (Liliová 10, tel. 02/2424–8793) is authentically Irish (it has Irish owners), with Guinness on tap and excellent food of the fish-and-chips persuasion. **U Malého Glena** (Karmelitská 23, tel. 02/535–8115) offers a popular bar and a stage for local and expat jazz, blues, and folk.

Rock Clubs

Prague's rock, alternative, and world-music scene is thriving. The cavernous **Palác Akropolis** (Kubelíkova 27, tel. 02/2271–2287), in the Žižkov neighborhood, has top Czech acts and major international world-music performers; as the name suggests, the space has an Acropolis theme. Hard-rock enthusiasts should check out the **Rock Café** (Národní 20, tel. 02/2491–4416). You can also slouch into the **Lucerna Music Bar** (Vodičkova 36, tel. 02/2421–7108) to catch popular Czech rock and funk bands and visiting acts.

For dance tracks, hip locals congregate at **Roxy** (Dlouhá 33, tel. 02/2481–0951). **Malostranská Beseda** (Malostranské nám. 21, tel. 02/539–024) is a dependable bet for sometimes bizarre but always good musical acts from around the country.

THE ARTS

Prague's cultural flair is legendary, and performances are sometimes booked far in advance by all sorts of Praguers. The concierge at your hotel may be able to reserve tickets for you. Otherwise, for the cheapest tickets go directly to the theater box office a few days in advance or immediately before a performance. Ticket agencies may charge higher prices than box offices do. **Ticketpro** (main branch: Salvátorská 10, tel. 02/2481–4020), with outlets all over town, accepts major credit cards. Another big agency is **Bohemia Ticket International** (Na Příkopě16, tel. 02/2421–5031, or Malé nám. 13, tel. 02/2422–7832). You can also purchase tickets at **American Express** (☞ Travel Agencies in Practical Information).

Film

If a film was made in the United States or Britain, the chances are good that it will be shown with Czech subtitles rather than dubbed. (Film titles, however, are usually translated into Czech, so your only clue to the movie's country of origin may be the poster used in advertisements.) Movies in the original language are normally indicated with the note *český mi titulky* (with Czech subtitles). Many downtown cinemas cluster near Wenceslas Square.

One of the largest movie theaters is **Blaník** (Václavské nám. 56, tel. 02/2221–0110). **Lucerna** (Vodičkova 36, tel. 02/2421–6972) is a classic picture palace in the shopping arcade of the same name. **Praha** (Václavské nám. 17, tel. 02/262–035) shows first-run features in the main hall and second-run films in a smaller screening room. Another central cinema with multiple screens is **Světozor** (Vodičkova 39, tel. 02/2494–7566). Prague's English-language publications carry film reviews and full timetables.

Music

Classical concerts are held all over the city throughout the year. One of the best orchestral venues is the resplendent Art Nouveau **Smetana Hall** (Obecní dům, nám. Republiky 5, tel. 02/2200–2100), home of the excellent Prague Symphony Orchestra and major venue for the annual Prague Spring music festival. **Dvořák Hall** (Rudolfinum, nám. Jana Palacha, tel. 02/2489–3111) is home to one of Central Europe's best orchestras, the Czech Philharmonic, led since 1998 by the Russian pianist-conductor Vladimir Ashkenazy. Frequent guest conductor Sir Charles Mackerras is a leading proponent of modern Czech music.

Performances also are held regularly at many of the city's **palaces and churches,** including the Garden on the Ramparts below Prague Castle (where the music comes with a view); both Churches of St. Nicholas; the Church of Sts. Simon and Jude on Dušní in the Old Town; the Church of St. James on Malá Štupartská, near Old Town Square; the Zrcadlová kaple (Mirror Chapel) in the Klementinum on Mariánské náměstí in the Old Town; and the Lobkowicz Palace at Prague Castle. If you're an organ-music buff, you'll most likely have your pick of recitals held in Prague's historic halls and churches. Popular programs are offered at the Church of St. Nicholas in the Lesser Quarter and the Church of St. James, where the organ plays amid a complement of Baroque statuary. Classical ensembles are the most common finds, and the standard of performance ranges from adequate to superb, though the programs tend to take few risks. Serious fans of Baroque music may have the opportunity to hear works of little-known Bohemian composers at these concerts. Some of the best chamber ensembles are the Talich Chamber Orchestra, the Prague Chamber Philharmonic (also known as the Prague Philharmonia), the Wihan Quartet, the Czech Trio, and the Agon contemporary music group.

Concerts at the **Villa Bertramka** (Mozartova 169, in Smíchov, tel. 02/540–012) emphasize the music of Mozart and his contemporaries.

Opera and Ballet

The Czech Republic has a strong operatic tradition. A great venue for a night at the opera is the plush **Národní divadlo** (National Theater; Národní třída 2, tel. 02/2490–1448). Performances at the **Statní Opera Praha** (State Opera House; Wilsonova 4, tel. 02/265–353), near the top of Wenceslas Square, can also be excellent.

Unlike during the Communist period, operas are almost always sung in their original tongue, and the repertoire offers plenty of Italian favorites as well as the Czech national composers Janáček, Dvořák, and Smetana. (Czech operas are supertitled in English.) These two theaters also often stage ballets. The historic **Stavovské divadlo** (Estates Theater; Ovocný trh 1, tel. 02/2421–5001), where *Don Giovanni* premiered in the 18th century, plays host to a mix of operas and dramatic works. Appropriate attire is recommended for all venues; the National and Estates theaters instituted a "no jeans" rule in 1998. Ticket prices have risen, but are still quite reasonable at 300 Kč–500 Kč (slightly more at the Estates Theater).

Puppet Shows

This traditional form of Czech popular entertainment has been given new life thanks to the productions mounted at the **Národní divadlo marionet** (National Marionette Theater; Žatecká 1, tel. 02/232–2536; in season, shows are also performed at Celetná 13). Children and adults alike can enjoy the hilarity and pathos of famous operas adapted for nonhuman "singers." The company's bread and butter is a production of Mozart's *Don Giovanni*.

Theater

A dozen or so professional theater companies play in Prague to ever-packed houses. Visiting the theater is a vital activity in Czech society, and the language barrier can't obscure the players' artistry. Nonverbal theater also abounds: not only tourist-friendly mime and "Black Light Theater"—a melding of live acting, mime, video, and stage trickery—but also serious (or incomprehensible) productions by top local and foreign troupes.

The famous **Laterna Magika** (Magic Lantern) puts on a multimedia extravaganza in the National Theater's ugly modern hall (Národní třída 4, tel. 02/2491–4129).

The popular **Archa Theater** (Na Poříčí 26, tel. 02/232–8800) offers avant-garde and experimental theater, music, and dance and has hosted world-class visiting ensembles such as the Royal Shakespeare Company. Several English-language theater groups operate sporadically. For complete listings, pick up a copy of the *Prague Post*.

In This Chapter

Updated by Ky Krauthamer

side trips to the bohemian spa towns

UNTIL WORLD WAR II, western Bohemia was the playground of Central Europe's rich and famous. Its three well-known spas, Karlovy Vary, Mariánské Lázně, and Františkovy Lázně (better known by their German names, Karlsbad, Marienbad, and Franzensbad, respectively), were the annual haunts of everybody who was anybody: Johann Wolfgang von Goethe, Ludwig van Beethoven, Karl Marx, and England's King Edward VII, to name but a few. Although strictly "proletarianized" in the Communist era, the spas still exude a nostalgic aura of a more elegant past and, unlike most of Bohemia, offer a basic tourist infrastructure that makes dining and lodging a pleasure.

The price categories in the listings below refer to the following charts; the first is for eating out, and the second, where to stay.

CATEGORY	PRICE*
$$$$	over $30
$$$	$15–$30
$$	$7–$15
$	under $7

*per person for a three-course meal, excluding wine and tip

CATEGORY	PRICE*
$$$$	over $100
$$$	$50–$100
$$	$25–$50
$	under $25

All prices are for a standard double room during peak season, including breakfast.

KARLOVY VARY

★ 132 km (79 mi) due west of Prague on Rte. 6 (E48).

Karlovy Vary, better known outside the Czech Republic by its German name, Karlsbad, is the most famous Bohemian spa. It is named for Emperor Charles IV, who allegedly happened upon the springs in 1358 while on a hunting expedition. As the story goes, the emperor's hound—chasing a harried stag—fell into a boiling spring and was scalded. Charles had the water tested and, familiar with spas in Italy, ordered baths to be established in the village of Vary. The spa reached its heyday in the 19th century, when royalty came here from all over Europe for treatment. The long list of those who "took the cure" includes Peter the Great, Goethe (no fewer than 13 times, according to a plaque on one house by the main spring), Schiller, Beethoven, and Chopin. Even Karl Marx, when he wasn't decrying wealth and privilege, spent time at the resort; he wrote some of *Das Kapital* here between 1874 and 1876.

After decades of neglect under the Communists that left many buildings crumbling behind their beautiful facades, the town leaders today face the daunting task of carving out a new role for Karlovy Vary, since few Czechs can afford to set aside weeks or months at a time for a leisurely cure. To raise some quick cash, many sanatoriums have turned to offering short-term accommodations to foreign visitors (at rather expensive rates). By the week or by the hour, "classical" spa procedures, laser treatments, plastic surgery, and even acupuncture are purveyed to German clients or to large numbers of Russians who have bought property in town in the last few years. For most visitors, though, it's enough simply to stroll the streets and parks and allow the eyes to feast awhile on the splendors of the past.

Whether you're arriving by bus, train, or car, your first view of the town on the approach from Prague will be of the ugly new section on the banks of the Ohře River. Don't despair: continue along the main road—following the signs to the Grandhotel Pupp—until you reach the lovely main street of the older spa area, situated gently astride the banks of the little Teplá ("Warm") River. (Drivers, note that driving through or parking in the main spa area is allowed only with a permit obtainable from your hotel.) The walk from the new town to the spa area is about 20 minutes. The **Historická čtvrt** (Historic District) is still largely intact. Tall 19th-century houses, boasting decorative and often eccentric facades, line the spa's proud riverside streets. Throughout you'll see colonnades full of people sipping the spa's hot sulfuric water from odd pipe-shape drinking cups. At night the streets fill with steam escaping from cracks in the earth, giving the town a slightly macabre feel.

Karlovy Vary's jarringly modern **Vřídelní kolonáda** (Vřídlo Colonnade) is built around the spring of the same name, the town's hottest and most dramatic gusher. The Vřídlo is indeed unique, shooting its scalding water to a height of some 40 ft. Walk inside the arcade to watch the hundreds of patients here take the famed Karlsbad drinking cure. They promenade somnambulistically up and down, eyes glazed, clutching drinking glasses filled periodically at one of the five "sources." The waters are said to be especially effective against diseases of the digestive and urinary tracts. They're also good for gout (which probably explains the spa's former popularity with royals!). If you want to join the crowds and take a sip, you can buy your own spouted cup from vendors within the colonnade.

To the right of the Vřídlo Colonnade are steps up to the white **Kostel Maří Magdaleny** (Church of Mary Magdalene). Designed by Kilian Ignaz Dientzenhofer (architect of the two Churches of St. Nicholas in Prague), this church is the best of the few Baroque buildings still standing in Karlovy Vary. *Moravská ul., no phone. Daily 9–6.*

The spa's centerpiece is just a couple minutes' walk along the river, back in the direction of the new town. The neo-Renaissance pillared hall **Mlýnská kolonáda** (Mill Colonnade), built from 1871 to 1881, has four springs: Rusalka, Libussa, Prince Wenceslas, and Millpond.

If you continue down the valley, you'll soon arrive at the very elegant **Sadová kolonáda** (Park Colonnade), a white, wrought iron construction. It was built in 1882 by the Viennese architectural duo of Fellner and Helmer, who sprinkled the Austro-Hungarian Empire with many such edifices during the late 19th century and who also designed the town's theater, the quaint wooden Tržní kolonáda (Market Colonnade) next to the Vřídlo Colonnade, and one of the old bathhouses.

The 20th century emerges at its most disturbing a little farther along the valley across the river, in the form of the huge, bunkerlike **Thermal Hotel**, built in the late 1960s. Although the building is a monstrosity, the view of Karlovy Vary from the rooftop pool is nothing short of spectacular. (The pool is open from 8 AM to 8 PM.) Even if you don't feel like a swim, it's worth taking the winding road up to the baths for the view. *I.P. Pavlova.*

From the Market Colonnade, a steep street called **Zámecký vrch** leads up to some other sights. A five-minute walk brings you to the redbrick Victorian **Kostel svatého Lukáše** (St. Luke's Church), at the intersection of Zámecký vrch and Petra Velikého, once used by the local English community. A few blocks farther along Petra Velikého street, you'll come to the splendid Russian Orthodox church **Kostel svatých Petra a**

Pavla (Church of Sts. Peter and Paul). Return to the Victorian church and take a sharp right uphill on the redbrick road. Then turn left onto a footpath through the woods, following the signs to **Jelení skok** (Stag's Leap). After a while you'll see steps leading up to a bronze statue of a deer looking over the cliffs, the symbol of Karlovy Vary. From here a winding path leads up to **Altán Jelení skok**, a little red gazebo opening onto a fabulous panorama.

. . . .

NEED A BREAK? Reward yourself for making the climb to Stag's Leap with a light meal at the nearby restaurant **Jelení skok.** You may have to pay an entrance fee if there is a live band (but you'll also get the opportunity to polka). If you don't want to walk up, you can drive up a signposted road from the Victorian church.

. . . .

It's not necessary to walk for one of the best views of the town. Above Stag's Leap is an observation tower, **rozhledna Diana,** accessible by funicular from behind the Grandhotel Pupp (☞ Where to Stay and Eat, *below*). There's an elevator to the top of the tower.

The town's most exclusive shopping clusters around the Grandhotel Pupp and back toward town along the river on Stará louka. Here too is the **Elefant** one of the last of a dying breed of sophisticated coffeehouses. This kind of elegant café is now a rarity, but happily the café as an institution is making a real comeback in the Czech Republic. *Stará louka 30*

Where to Stay and Eat

$$$$ **DVOŘÁK.** Consider a splurge here if you're longing for Western
★ standards of service and convenience. Opened in late 1990, this Austrian-owned hotel occupies three renovated town houses that are just a five-minute walk from the main spas. If possible, request a room with a bay-window view of the town. Spa treatments here run to about $750 per person per week in the high season. *Nová*

louka 11, 360 21, tel. 017/322–4145, fax 017/322–2814. 76 rooms, 3
suites. Restaurant, café, pool, beauty salon, massage, sauna, exercise
room, casino. AE, DC, MC, V. www.hotel-dvorak.cz

$$$–$$$$ **GRANDHOTEL PUPP.** This enormous hotel with a 215-year history
★ is one of Karlovy Vary's landmarks—it's also one of Central
Europe's most famous resorts. Standards and service slipped
under the Communists (when the hotel was known as the Moskva),
but the highly professional management has more than made up
for the decades of neglect. Some guest rooms are furnished in
18th-century period style. The vast public rooms exude the very
best taste, circa 1913, when the present building was completed.
Every July, the Pupp becomes a temporary home base for
international movie stars who come to the Karlovy Vary
International Film Festival. (The adjacent Parkhotel Pupp, under
the same management, is an affordable alternative to the
Grandhotel.) Breakfast costs 375 Kč extra. Mírové nám. 2, 360 91,
tel. 017/310–9111, fax 017/310–9620 or 017/322–4032. Grandhotel:
75 rooms, 34 suites. Parkhotel: 108 rooms, 6 suites. 4 restaurants, lounge,
sauna, exercise room, casino, 2 nightclubs, parking (fee). AE, DC, MC, V.
www.pupp.com

$$$ **ELWA.** Renovations have successfully integrated modern comforts
into this older, elegant spa resort located midway between the
old and new towns. Modern features include clean, comfortable
rooms with contemporary furnishings such as overstuffed chairs.
There's also an on-site fitness center. The spa specializes in
digestive diseases. Zahradní 29, 360 01, tel. 017/322–8472, fax 017/
322–8473. 10 rooms, 7 suites. Restaurant, bar, beauty salon, health club.
AE, MC, V.

$$$ **EMBASSY.** This cozy, sophisticated wine restaurant, conveniently
located near the Grandhotel Pupp, serves an innovative menu by
local standards. Tagliatelle with smoked salmon in cream sauce
makes an excellent main course, as does roast duck with cabbage
and dumplings. The wine list features Czech varieties like the dry

whites Rulandské bílé and Ryzlink Rýnský (the latter being the domestic version of the Riesling grape) and some pricey imports. *Nová louka 21, tel. 017/322–1161. AE, DC, MC, V.*

$$$ RŮŽE. More than adequately comfortable and well-priced given its location smack in the center of the spa district, this is a good choice for travelers who prefer a hotel to a pension or private room. *I.P. Pavlova 1, 360 01, tel./fax 017/322–1846 or 017/322–1853. 20 rooms. Restaurant. AE, V.*

$$ KAREL IV. Its location atop an old castle tower not far from the Market Colonnade gives diners the best view in town. Good renditions of traditional Czech standbys—bramborák (potato pancake) and chicken breast with peaches—are served in small, secluded dining areas that are particularly intimate after sunset. *Zámecký vrch 2, tel. 017/322–7255. AE, MC, V.*

Shopping

In western Bohemia, Karlovy Vary is best known to glass enthusiasts as the home of **Moser** (Tržiště 7, tel. 017/323–5303), one of the world's leading producers of crystal and decorative glassware. A number of outlets for lesser-known, although also high-quality, makers of glass and porcelain can be found along Stará louka. For excellent buys in porcelain, try **Karlovarský porcelán** (Tržiště 27, tel. 017/322–5660).

A cheaper but nonetheless unique gift from Karlovy Vary would be a bottle of the ubiquitous bittersweet (and potent) **Becherovka,** a liqueur produced by the town's own Jan Becher distillery. Another neat gift would be one of the pipe-shape ceramic drinking cups used to take the drinking cure at spas; you can find them at the colonnades. You can also buy boxes of tasty *oplatky* (wafers), sometimes covered with chocolate, at shops in all of the spa towns.

Outdoor Activities and Sports

Karlovy Vary's warm open-air public pool on top of the **Thermal Hotel** (I.P. Pavlova) offers the unique experience of swimming comfortably even in the coolest weather; the view over the town is outstanding. Marked **hiking trails** snake across the beech-and-pine-covered hills that surround the town on three sides. The **Karlovy Vary Golf Club** is just out of town on the road to Prague.

Nightlife and the Arts

In Karlovy Vary, the upscale action centers on the two nightclubs and the casino of the **Grandhotel Pupp** (☞ Where to Stay and Eat, *above*). **Club Propaganda** (Jaltská 7, tel. 017/323–3792) is Karlovy Vary's best venue for live rock and new music. The Karlovy Vary Symphony Orchestra plays regularly at **LázněIII** (Mlýnské nábř. 5, tel. 017/322–5641).

CHEB

42 km (26 mi) southwest of Karlovy Vary.

Known for centuries by its German name of Eger, the old town of Cheb lies on the border with Germany in the far west of the Czech Republic. The town has been a fixture of Bohemia since 1322 (when it was handed over to King Jan, or Johann, as thanks for his support of a Bavarian prince), but as you walk around the beautiful medieval square, it's difficult not to think you're in Germany. The tall merchants' houses surrounding the main square, with their long, red-tile, sloping roofs dotted with windows like droopy eyelids, are more Germanic in style than anything else in Bohemia. You'll also hear a lot of German on the streets—more from the many German visitors than from the town's residents.

Germany took full possession of the town in 1938 under the terms of the notorious Munich Pact. But following World War II,

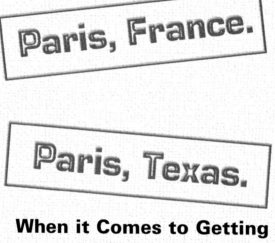

Paris, France.

Paris, Texas.

When it Comes to Getting Local Currency at an ATM, Same Thing.

Whether you're in Yosemite or Yemen, using your Visa® card or ATM card with the PLUS symbol is the easiest and most convenient way to get local currency. For example, let's say you're in France. When you make a withdrawal, using your secured PIN, it's dispensed in francs, but is debited from your account in U.S. dollars. This makes it easy to take advantage of favorable exchange rates. And if you need help finding one of Visa's 627,000 ATMs in 127 countries worldwide, visit **visa.com/pd/atm**. We'll make finding an ATM as easy as finding the Eiffel Tower, the Pyramids or even the Grand Canyon.

It's Everywhere You Want To Be®

SEE THE WORLD
IN FULL COLOR

Fodor's Exploring Guides bring all the great sights vividly to life with hundreds of photographs, fascinating historical background, and colorful anecdotes. Detailed maps and practical information keep you headed in the right direction.

Pair a Fodor's Exploring Guide with your trusted Fodor's Pocket Guide for a complete planning package.

Fodor's EXPLORING GUIDES

At bookstores everywhere.

virtually the entire German population was expelled, and the Czech name of Cheb was officially adopted. A more notorious German connection emerged in the years following the 1989 revolution: Cheb, like other border towns, became an unofficial center of prostitution. Don't be startled to see young women, provocatively dressed, lining the highways and roads into town.

The **statue** in the middle of the central square, náměstí Krále Jiřího z Poděbrad, similar to the Roland statues you see throughout Bohemia and attesting to the town's royal privileges, represents the town hero, Wastel of Eger. Look carefully at his right foot, and you'll see a small man holding a sword and a head—this shows the town had its own judge and executioner.

On the lower part of náměstí Krále Jiřího z Poděbrad are two rickety groups of timbered medieval buildings, 11 houses in all, divided by a narrow alley. The houses, forming the area known as **Špalíček,** date from the 13th century and were home to many Jewish merchants. **Židovská ulice** (Jews' Street), running uphill to the left of the Špalíček, served as the actual center of the ghetto. Note the small alley running off to the left of Židovská. This calm street, with the seemingly inappropriate name ulička Zavražděných (Lane of the Murdered), was the scene of an outrageous act of violence in 1350: Pressures had been building for some time between Jews and Christians. Incited by an anti-Semitic bishop, the townspeople finally chased the Jews into the street, closed off both ends, and massacred them. Now only the name attests to the slaughter.

NEED A BREAK? Cheb's main square abounds with cafés and little restaurants, all offering a fairly uniform menu of schnitzel and sauerbraten aimed at visiting Germans. The **Kavárna Špalíček,** nestled in the Špalíček buildings, is one of the better choices and has the added advantage of a unique architectural setting.

History buffs, particularly those interested in the Hapsburgs, will want to visit the **Chebské muzeum** (Cheb Museum) in the Pachelbel House on the main square. It was in this house that the great general of the Thirty Years' War, Albrecht von Wallenstein, was murdered in 1634 on the orders of his own emperor, the Hapsburg Ferdinand II, who was provoked by Wallenstein's increasing power and rumors of treason. According to legend, Wallenstein was on his way to the Saxon border to enlist support to fight the Swedes when his own officers barged into his room and stabbed him through the heart with a stave. In his memory, the stark bedroom with its four-poster bed and dark red velvet curtains has been left as it was. (The story also inspired playwright Friedrich Schiller to write the *Wallenstein* trilogy; he planned the work while living at the top of the square at No. 2.) The museum is interesting in its own right: It has a selection from the Wallenstein family picture gallery, a section on the history of Cheb, and a collection of minerals (including one discovered by Goethe). *Nám. Krále Jiřího z Poděbrad 3, tel. 0166/422–246. 40 Kč. Mar.–Dec., Tues.–Sun. 9– noon and 1–5.*

The **art gallery** in the bright yellow Baroque house near the top of the square offers a well-chosen sampling of 20th-century Czech art. One of the country's best-known galleries of photography, **Gallery 4,** is just off the square at Kamenná 2.

The plain but imposing **Kostel svatého Mikuláše** (Church of St. Nicholas) was begun in 1230, when the church belonged to the Order of the Teutonic Knights. You can still see Romanesque windows on the towers; renovations throughout the centuries added an impressive Gothic portal and a Baroque interior. Just inside the Gothic entrance is a wonderfully faded plaque commemorating the diamond jubilee of Hapsburg emperor Franz Joseph in 1908. *Kostelní nám., no phone.*

Follow Křižovnická, behind the Church of St. Nicholas, up to **Chebský hrad** (Cheb Castle), which stands on a cliff overlooking the Ohře River. The castle—now a ruin—was built in the late 12th century for Holy Roman Emperor Frederick Barbarossa. The square black tower was built with blocks of lava taken from the nearby Komorní Hůrka volcano; the redbrick walls are 17th-century additions. Inside the castle grounds is the carefully restored double-decker Romanesque chapel, notable for the many lovely columns with heads carved into their capitals. The rather dark ground floor was used by commoners. The bright, ornate top floor was reserved for the emperor and his family, who entered via a wooden bridge leading to the royal palace. *Hradní ul., tel. 0166/422–942. 20 Kč. Apr. and Oct., Tues.–Sun. 9–4; May and Sept., Tues.–Sun. 9–5; June–Aug., Tues.–Sun. 9–6.*

Where to Stay and Eat

Cheb's hotels have failed to keep pace with the times. For a short stay, a room in a **private home** is a better bet. The city tourist information center (☞ *Visitor Information in Practical Information*) can arrange accommodations. Several houses along Přemysla Otakara street north of the city have rooms available, and the hotels in Františkovy Lázně (☞ *below*) are just a few minutes' drive or train ride away.

$$ EVA. Of the many restaurants opened on and around the main square since the tourism boom began in the early 1990s, Eva is certainly one of the best. A decent array of mostly Czech and German dishes is served by a troop of attentive waiters. *Jateční 4, tel. 0166/422–498. No credit cards.*

FRANTIŠKOVY LÁZNĚ

6 km (4 mi) from Cheb.

This little spa town couldn't be a more distinct contrast to nearby Cheb's slightly seedy, hustling air and medieval streetscapes. You might like to ease the transition by walking the path, indicated with red markers, from Cheb's main square

westward along the river and then north past **Komorní Hůrka.**
The extinct volcano is now a tree-covered hill, but excavations on
one side have laid bare the rock, and one tunnel is still open.
Goethe instigated and took part in the excavations, and you can
still—though barely—make out a relief of the poet carved into
the rock face.

Františkovy Lázně, or Franzensbad, the smallest of the three
main Bohemian spas, isn't really in the same league as the other
two (Karlovy Vary and Mariánské Lázně). Built on a more modest
scale at the start of the 19th century, the town's ubiquitous
kaiser-yellow buildings have been spruced up after their neglect
under the previous regime and now present cheerful facades,
almost too bright for the few strollers. The poorly kept parks and
the formal yet human-scale neoclassical architecture retain
much of their former charm. Overall, a pleasing torpor reigns in
Františkovy Lázně. There is no town to speak of, just **Národní
ulice,** the main street, which leads down into the spa park. The
waters, whose healing properties were already known in the
16th century, are used primarily for treating heart problems—
and infertility, hence the large number of young women
wandering the grounds.

The most interesting sight in town may be the small **Lázeňský
muzeum** (Spa Museum), just off Národní ulice. There is a
wonderful collection of spa-related antiques, including copper
bathtubs and a turn-of-the-20th-century exercise bike called a
Velotrab. The guest books provide an insight into the
cosmopolitan world of pre–World War I Central Europe. The
book for 1812 contains the entry "Ludwig van Beethoven,
composer from Vienna." *Ul. Doktora Pohoreckého 8, tel. 0166/542–
344. 20 Kč. Tues.–Fri. 10–5, weekends 10–4 (usually closed mid-Dec.–
mid-Jan.).*

The main spring, **Františkův pramen,** is under a little gazebo
filled with brass pipes. The colonnade to the left was decorated
with a bust of Lenin that was replaced in 1990 by a memorial to

the American liberation of the town in April 1945. The oval neo-Classical temple just beyond the spring (amazingly, not painted yellow and white) is the **Glauberova dvorana** (Glauber Pavilion), where several springs bubble up into glass cases. *Národní ul.*

NEED A BREAK? Only insipid pop music (the scourge of eating and drinking places everywhere in the country) interrupts the cheerful atmosphere of the little café of the **Slovan** (☞ Where to Stay and Eat, *below*) on Národní. The tiny gallery and lively frescoes make it a great spot for cake, coffee, or drinks.

Where to Stay and Eat

Most of the establishments in town do a big trade in spa patients, who generally stay for several weeks. Spa treatments usually require a medical check and cost substantially more than the normal room charge. Walk-in treatment can be arranged at some hotels or at the information center (☞ Visitor Information in Practical Information). Signs around town advertise massage therapy and other treatments for casual visitors.

$$$ TŘI LILIE. Reopened in 1995 after an expensive refitting, the "Three Lilies," which once accommodated the likes of Goethe and Metternich, immediately reestablished itself as the most comfortable spa hotel in town. It is thoroughly elegant, from guest rooms to brasserie. *Národní 3, tel./fax 0166/542–415. 31 rooms. Restaurant, brasserie, café. AE, MC, V.*

$$ CENTRUM. Rooms in this barnlike building are well appointed if a bit sterile. Still, it is among the best-run hotels in town and only a short walk from the main park and central spas. *Anglická 392, 351 01, tel. 0166/543–156, fax 0166/543–157. 30 rooms. Restaurant, bar. AE, MC, V.*

$$ SLOVAN. This gracious place is the perfect complement to this
★ relaxed little town. The eccentricity of the original turn-of-the-20th-
century design survived a thorough renovation during the 1970s.
The airy rooms are clean and comfortable, and some have a
balcony overlooking the main street. The main-floor restaurant
serves above-average Czech dishes such as tasty *svíčková* (beef
sirloin in a citrusy cream sauce) and roast duck. *Národní 5, 351 01,
tel. 0166/542–841, fax 0166/542–843. 25 rooms, 19 with bath.
Restaurant, bar, café. AE, MC, V.*

MARIÁNSKÉ LÁZNĚ
★ *30 km (18 mi) southeast of Cheb, 47 km (29 mi) south of Karlovy Vary.*

Your expectations of what a spa resort should be may come
nearest to fulfillment here. It's far larger and more active than
Františkovy Lázně and greener and quieter than Karlovy Vary (☞
above). This was the spa favored by Britain's Edward VII. Goethe
and Chopin also repaired here frequently. Mark Twain, on a visit
to the spa in 1892, labeled the town a "health factory" and
couldn't get over how new everything looked. Indeed, at that
time everything was new. The sanatoriums, most built during
the 19th century in a confident, outrageous mixture of "neo"
styles, fan out impressively around a finely groomed oblong
park. Cure takers and curiosity seekers alike parade through the
Empire-style Cross Spring pavilion and the long colonnade near
the top of the park. Buy a spouted drinking cup (available at the
colonnades) and join the rest of the sippers taking the drinking
cure. Be forewarned, though: the waters from the Rudolph,
Ambrose, and Caroline springs, though harmless, all have a
noticeable diuretic effect. For this reason they're used
extensively in treating disorders of the kidney and bladder. For
information on spa treatments, inquire at the main **spa offices**
(Masarykova 22, tel. 0165/623–061). Walk-in treatment can be
arranged at the **Nové Lázně** (New Spa; Reitenbergerova 53, tel.
0165/644–111).

A stay in Mariánské Lázně can be healthful even without special treatment. Special walking trails of all difficulty levels surround the resort in all directions. The best advice is simply to put on comfortable shoes, buy a hiking map, and head out. One of the country's few golf courses lies about 3 km (2 mi) to the east of town. Hotels can also help to arrange special activities, such as tennis and horseback riding. For the less intrepid, a simple stroll around the gardens, with a few deep breaths of the town's famous air, is enough to restore a healthy sense of perspective.

Where to Stay and Eat

The best place to look for private lodgings is along Paleckého ulice and Hlavní třída, south of the main spa area. Private accommodations can also be found in the neighboring villages of Zádub and Závišín in the woods to the east of town.

$$$$ EXCELSIOR. This lovely older hotel is on the main street and is convenient to the spas and colonnade. Rooms have traditional cherry-wood furniture and marble bathrooms, and the views over the town are enchanting. The staff is friendly and multilingual. While the food in the restaurant is only average, the romantic setting provides adequate compensation. *Hlavní třída 121, 353 01, tel. 0165/622–705, fax 0165/625–346. 64 rooms. Restaurant, café, massage, sauna. AE, DC, MC, V.*

$$$ BOHEMIA. At this gracious, century-old hotel, beautiful crystal ★ chandeliers in the main hall set the stage for a comfortable and elegant stay. The crisp beige-and-white rooms let you spread out and *really* unpack; they're spacious and high ceilinged. (If you want to indulge, request one of the enormous suites overlooking the park.) The helpful staff can arrange spa treatments and horseback riding. *Hlavní třída 100, 353 01, tel. 0165/623–251, fax 0165/622–943. 73 rooms, 4 suites. Restaurant, café, lounge. AE, MC, V.*

$$$ HOTEL GOLF. Book in advance to secure a room at this stately villa situated 3½ km (2 mi) out of town on the road to Karlovy Vary. The large, open rooms are cheery and modern. The restaurant on the main floor is excellent, but the big draw is the 18-hole golf course on the premises, one of the few in the Czech Republic. The course was opened in 1905 by King Edward VII. *Zádub 55, 353 01, tel. 0165/622–651 or 0165/622–652, fax 0165/622–655. 25 rooms. Restaurant, pool, 18-hole golf course, tennis court, nightclub. AE, DC, MC, V.*

$$ FILIP. This bustling wine bar is where locals come to find relief from the sometimes large horde of tourists. There's a tasty selection of traditional Czech dishes—mainly pork, grilled meats, and steaks. *Poštovní 96, tel. 0165/626–161. No credit cards.*

$$ KOLIBA. This combination hunting lodge and wine tavern, set in ★ the woods roughly 10 minutes on foot from the spas, is an excellent alternative to the hotel restaurants in town. Grilled meats and shish kebabs, plus tankards of Moravian wine (try the dry, cherry red Rulandské červené), are served with traditional gusto while fiddlers play rousing Moravian tunes. *Dusíkova 592, in the direction of Karlovy Vary, tel. 0165/625–169. V.*

Nightlife and the Arts

The West Bohemian Symphony Orchestra performs regularly in the New Spa (Nové Lázně, ☞ *above*). The town's annual Chopin festival each August brings in pianists from around Europe to perform the Polish composer's works.

Casino Lil (Anglická 336, tel. 0165/623–293) is open daily 2 PM– 7 AM. For late-night drinks, try the **Hotel Golf** (☞ Where to Stay and Eat, *above*), which has a good nightclub with dancing in season.

PLZEŇ

92 km (55 mi) west of Prague.

The sprawling industrial city of Plzeňis hardly a tourist mecca, but it's worth stopping off for an hour or two on the way back to

Prague. Two sights here are of particular interest to beer fanatics. The first is the **Pilsner Urquell Brewery,** to the east of the city near the railway station. The beer was created in 1842 using the excellent Plzeň water, a special malt fermented on the premises, and hops grown in the region around Žatec. On a group tour of the 19th-century redbrick building you can taste the valuable brew, exported around the world. Tours in English and German are offered weekdays at 12:30 PM (sometimes also at 2 PM in the summer). You can only visit via the tour. *U Prazdroje 7, tel. 019/706–1111. 70 Kč.*

NEED A
BREAK?
You can continue drinking and find some cheap traditional grub at the large **Na Spilce** beer hall just inside the brewery gates. The pub is open daily from 10 AM to 10 PM.

The second stop on the beer tour is the **Pivovarské muzeum** (Brewery Museum), in a late-Gothic malt house one block northeast of náměstí Republiky (☞ *below*). All kinds of paraphernalia trace the region's brewing history, including the horse-drawn carts used to haul the kegs. *Veleslavinova 6, tel. 019/ 723–5574. 40 Kč. Daily 10–6.*

The city's architectural attractions center on the main **náměstí Republiky** (Republic Square). The square is dominated by the enormous Gothic **Chrám svatého Bartoloměje** (Church of St. Bartholomew). Both the square and the church towers hold size records: the former is the largest in Bohemia and the latter, at 335 ft, the tallest in the Czech Republic. Around the square, mixed in with its good selection of stores, are a variety of other architectural jewels, including the town hall, adorned with sgraffiti and built in the Renaissance style by Italian architects during the town's heyday in the 16th century. The Moorish **synagogue,** one of the largest in Europe, is four blocks west of the square, just outside the green strip that circles the old town.

Distance Conversion Chart

Kilometers/Miles

To change kilometers (km) to miles (mi), multiply km by .621.
To change mi to km, multiply mi by 1.61.

km to mi	mi to km
1 = .62	1 = 1.6
2 = 1.2	2 = 3.2
3 = 1.9	3 = 4.8
4 = 2.5	4 = 6.4
5 = 3.1	5 = 8.1
6 = 3.7	6 = 9.7
7 = 4.3	7 = 11.3
8 = 5.0	8 = 12.9

Meters/Feet

To change meters (m) to feet (ft), multiply m by 3.28.
To change ft to m, multiply ft by .305.

m to ft	ft to m
1 = 3.3	1 = .30
2 = 6.6	2 = .61
3 = 9.8	3 = .92
4 = 13.1	4 = 1.2
5 = 16.4	5 = 1.5
6 = 19.7	6 = 1.8
7 = 23.0	7 = 2.1
8 = 26.2	8 = 2.4

Where to Stay and Eat

$$$ CENTRAL. This angular 1960s structure is recommendable for its sunny rooms, friendly staff, and great location, right on the main square. Indeed, even such worthies as Czar Alexander of Russia stayed here in the days when the hotel was a charming inn known as the Golden Eagle. *Nám. Republiky 33, 305 31, tel. 019/722–6757, fax 019/722–6064. 77 rooms. Restaurant, bar, café. AE, DC, MC, V.*

$$$ CONTINENTAL. Just five minutes on foot from the main square, the fin-de-siècle Continental remains a good choice, even though the hotel is slightly run down and the rooms, though large, are exceedingly plain. The restaurant, however, serves dependably satisfying traditional Czech dishes such as *cibulka* (onion soup) and *svíčková* (beef sirloin in a citrusy cream sauce). *Zbojnická 8, 305 31, tel. 019/723–6477, fax 019/722–1746. 46 rooms, 23 with bath or shower. Restaurant, café. AE, DC, MC, V.*

In This Chapter

Updated by Ky Krauthamer

where to stay

THE NUMBER OF HOTELS AND PENSIONS has increased dramatically throughout the Czech Republic, in step with the influx of tourists. A slow rise in lodging standards continues, but at all but the most expensive hotels standards lag behind those of Germany and Austria—as do prices. In most of the $$$$ and $$$ hotels, you can expect to find a restaurant and an exchange bureau on or near the premises. During the peak season (in Prague, April through October and the Christmas, New Year, and Easter holidays) reservations are absolutely imperative; for the remainder of the year they are highly recommended. Many hotels in Prague go by a three-season system: the lowest rates are charged from December through February, excluding Christmas (at some hotels) and New Year's (at all hotels), when high-season rates are charged; the middle season includes March, November, and often July and August; and spring and fall bring the highest rates. Easter sees higher-than-high-season rates, and some hotels up the price for other holidays and trade fairs. It always pays to ask first.

Hotel prices, in general, remain high. Some Prague hotels reduce rates slightly in July and August, when many European travelers prefer to head for the beaches. Better value can often be found at private pensions or at bare-bones hostels, now a popular means of circumventing Prague's summer lodging crunch; many now stay open all year.

A private room or apartment can be another cheaper and more interesting alternative to a hotel. You'll find agencies offering such accommodations all over Prague, including at the main train station (Hlavní nádraží), Holešovice station (Nádraží Holešovice), and at Ruzyně Airport. These bureaus normally are staffed with people who can speak some English, and most can book rooms in hotels and pensions as well as private accommodations. Rates for private rooms start at around $15 per person per night and can go much higher for better-quality rooms. In general, there is no fee, but you may need to try several bureaus to find the accommodation you want. Ask to see a photo of the room before accepting it, and be sure to pinpoint its location on a map—you don't want to wind up in an inconveniently distant location. You may be approached by (usually) men in the stations hawking rooms, and while these deals aren't always rip-offs, you should be wary of them. **Prague Information Service** (☞ Visitor Information in Practical Information) arranges lodging from all of its central offices, including the branch in the main train station, which is in the booth marked TURISTICKÉ INFORMACE on the left side of the main hall as you exit the station.

The bluntly named **Accommodation Service** (Haštalská 7, tel. 02/231–0202 or 0602/210–515, fax 02/231–6640) is a small but efficient agency that specializes in Old Town apartments at about 2,000 Kč for either one or two people and also arranges less costly rooms farther from the center. It's open daily between April and October from 9 to 7 and from November to March 9 to 1 and 2 to 6 (Sunday 9 to 1). Another helpful agency is **Hello Ltd.** (Senovážné nám. 3, tel./fax 02/2421–2647 or 02/2421–4212), open daily 9 AM– 9 PM (weekdays 8–7 in the off-season); it's a 10-minute walk from the main train station. Both these agencies provide car or minivan transfers from the airport and train stations.

CATEGORY	PRICE*
$$$$	over $200
$$$	$100–$200
$$	$50–$100
$	under $50

*All prices are for a standard double room during peak season, including breakfast.

Czech hotels set their own star ratings, which more or less match the international star system. Often you can book rooms—both at hotels and in private homes—through visitor bureaus. Otherwise, try calling or writing the hotel directly. Keep in mind that in many hotels, except at the deluxe level, a "double" bed means two singles that can be pushed together. (Single-mattress double beds are generally not available.) Unless otherwise noted, breakfast is included in the rate.

STARÉ MĚSTO (OLD TOWN)

$$$$ GRAND HOTEL BOHEMIA. This beautifully refurbished Art Nouveau town palace sits across the street from Obecní dùm (Municipal House), near the Prašná brána (Powder Tower). During the Communist era it was a nameless, secure hideaway for ranking foreign party members. Once restored to private hands, the Austrian owners opted for a muted, modern decor in the rooms but left the sumptuous Boccaccio ballroom in its faux-rococo glory. In the rooms, sweeping, long drapes frame spectacular views of the Old Town. Each room's amenities include a fax, trouser press, and answering machine. *Královodvorská 4, 110 00 Prague 1, tel. 02/2480–4111, fax 02/232–9545. 73 rooms, 5 suites. Restaurant, bar, café, in-room safes, minibars, no-smoking floor, meeting rooms. AE, DC, MC, V. austria-hotels.co.at*

$$$ MAXIMILIAN. Oversize beds, classic French cherry-wood furniture, and thick drapes make for a relaxing stay in this luxurious hotel. A relatively new property (opened in 1995), it's located on a

Apollo, 25	Dùm U Červeného Lva, 5	Mepro, 10	Penzion Sprint, 2
Astra, 27		Meteor Plaza, 17	Petr, 8
Axa, 22	Grand Hotel Bohemia, 18	Olšanka, 16	Romantik Hotel U Raka, 3
Balkan, 11	Harmony, 23	Opera, 24	Salvator, 21
Bern, 15	Kampa, 7	Palace, 14	Savoy, 4
Central, 19	Kinsky Garden, 9	Pension Louda, 26	U Tří Pštrosů, 6
City Hotel Moran, 12	Maximilian, 20	Pension Unitas, 13	
Diplomat, 1			

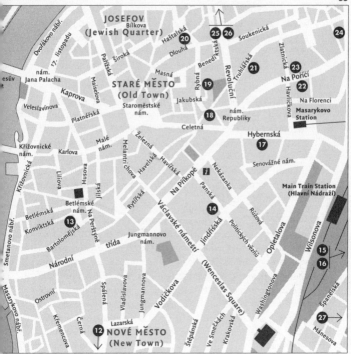

JOSEFOV
Bílkova
(Jewish Quarter)

25 26 Soukenická

Haštalská 20

Dvořákovo nábř. 17. listopadu

Dlouhá

24

Pařížská Široká

Benedikt

Revoluční

Zlatnická

21

23

nám. Jana Palacha

Maiselova

Masná

Rybná

Trohlářská

Na Poříčí 22

Veleslavínova

Kaprova

STARÉ MĚSTO
(Old Town)

19

Havlíčkova

Na Florenci

Platnéřská

Staroměstské
nám.

Jakubská

Masarykovo
Station

Křižovnické nám.

Karlova

Malé nám.

Železná

18

Celetná

nám.
Republiky

Hybernská

17

Smetanovo nábř.

Lilíová

Husova

Betlémské nám.

Melantrichova

Havelská

Havířská

Na Příkopě

i

Nekázanka

Senovážné nám.

Main Train Station
(Hlavní Nádraží)

13

Bartolomějská

Betlémská
Konviktská

Na Perštýně

Rytířská

Panská

14

Růžová

Opletalova

Wilsonova

Národní

Jungmannovo
nám.

třída

Václavské náměstí

Jindřišská

Politických vězňů

15
16

Ostrovní

Spálená

Vladislavova

Jungmannova

Vodičkova

(Wenceslas Square)

Washingtonova

Španělská

Masarykovo nábř.

Křemencova

černá

12

Lazarská

NOVÉ MĚSTO
(New Town)

Štěpánská

Ve Smečkách

Krakovská

27

Mánesova

peaceful square, well away from traffic, noise, and crowds, yet within easy walking distance to Old Town Square and Pařížská street. There are fax machines and satellite TVs in every room. *Haštalská 14, 110 00 Prague 1, tel. 02/2180–6111, fax 02/2180–6110. 72 rooms. Breakfast room, in-room safes, minibars, meeting rooms, no-smoking rooms, parking (fee). AE, DC, MC, V.*

$$ CENTRAL. This hotel lives up to its name, with a site on a relatively quiet side street near Celetná ulice and náměstí Republiky (Republic Square). Recent "improvements" raised prices more than the quality level, leaving the hallways as drab and the rooms as sparely furnished as ever (most lack TVs), but it remains perhaps the least expensive full-service hotel in the Old Town. *Rybná 8, 110 00 Prague 1, tel. 02/2481–2041, fax 02/232–8404. 62 rooms, 4 suites. Restaurant. AE, DC, MC, V.*

$ PENSION UNITAS. Now operated by the Christian charity Unitas, the spartan rooms of this former convent used to serve as interrogation cells for the Communist secret police. (Václav Havel was once a "guest.") Today conditions are much more comfortable, though the ambience is more that of a hostel than a pension. There's a common (but clean) bathroom on each floor. You'll need to reserve well in advance, even in the off-season. No smoking is allowed. Note that there is an adjacent three-star hotel, Cloister Inn, using the same location and phone number; when calling, specify the pension. *Bartolomějská 9, 110 00 Prague 1, tel. 02/232–7700, fax 02/232–7709. 40 rooms, none with bath. Restaurant. No credit cards.*

MALÁ STRANA (LESSER QUARTER)

$$$ DŮM U ČERVENÉHO LVA. ★ On the Lesser Quarter's main, historic thoroughfare, a five-minute walk from Prague Castle's front gates, the "Baroque House at the Red Lion" is an intimate, immaculately kept hotel. Guest rooms have parquet floors, 17th-century painted-beam ceilings, superb antiques, and all-white bathrooms with brass fixtures. The two top-floor rooms can double as a suite. Note that there is no elevator, and the stairs are steep. *Nerudova 41, 118 00 Prague 1. tel. 02/5753–3832 or 02/5753–3833, fax 02/5753–2746. 5 rooms, 3 suites. 2 restaurants, bar, in-room safes, minibars. AE, DC, MC, V. www.hotel-lev.com*

$$$ KAMP A. ★ This early Baroque armory turned hotel is tucked away on an abundantly picturesque street at the southern end of the Lesser Quarter, just off Kampa Island. The bucolic setting and comparatively low rates make the hotel one of the city's better bargains. Note the late-Gothic vaulting in the massive dining room. *Všehrdova 16, 118 00 Prague 1, tel. 02/5732–0508 or 02/5732–0404, fax 02/5732–0262. 85 rooms. Restaurant, minibars. AE, MC, V.*

$$$ U TŘÍ PŠTROSÙ. The location could not be better: a romantic corner just a stone's throw from the river and within arms' reach of the Charles Bridge. The airy rooms of the centuries-old building still have their original oak-beam ceilings and antique furniture, and many have views over the river. Massive walls keep out the noise of the crowds on the bridge. An excellent in-house restaurant serves traditional Czech dishes to guests and nonguests alike. Rates drop slightly in July and August—probably because there's no air-conditioning, though the building's thick walls help keep it cool. *Dražického nám. 12, 118 00 Prague 1, tel. 02/5753–2410, fax 02/5753–3217. 14 rooms, 4 suites. Restaurant. AE, DC, MC, V. www.utripstrosu.cz*

HRADČANY

$$$$ SAVOY. ★ A restrained yellow Jugendstil facade conceals one of the city's most luxurious small hotels. The former budget hotel was gutted and lavishly refurbished in the mid-1990s. A harmonious maroon-and-mahogany color scheme carries through the public spaces and the rooms, some of which are furnished in purely modern style while others have a rococo look. The Restaurant Hradčany is one of the city's best hotel dining rooms. The only drawback: although Prague Castle is just up the road, none of the rooms have a view of it. *Keplerova 6, 118 00 Prague 6, tel. 02/2430–2430, fax 02/2430–2128. 55 rooms, 6 suites. Restaurant, café, in-room*

safes, minibars, sauna, exercise room, meeting rooms. AE, DC, MC, V.
www.hotel-savoy.cz

$$$ ROMANTIK HOTEL U RAKA. This private guest house, since 1997
★ a member of the Romantik Hotels & Restaurants organization,
has a quiet location on the ancient, winding streets of Nový Svět,
just behind the Loreto Church and a 10-minute walk from Prague
Castle. One side of the 18th-century building presents a rare
example of half-timbering, and the rooms sustain the country feel
with heavy furniture reminiscent of a Czech farmhouse. There are
only six rooms, but if you can get a reservation (try at least a
month in advance), you will have a wonderful base for exploring
Prague. Černínská 10/93, 118 00 Prague 1, tel. 02/2051–1100, fax 02/
2051–0511. 5 rooms, 1 suite. Breakfast room. AE, MC, V. www.
romantikhotels.com

NOVÉ MĚSTO (NEW TOWN)

$$$$ PALACE. For the well-heeled, this is Prague's most coveted
★ address—a muted, pistachio green Art Nouveau building perched
on a busy corner only a block from Wenceslas Square. The hotel's
spacious, well-appointed rooms, each with a white-marble
bathroom, are dressed in velvety pinks and greens cribbed straight
from an Alfons Mucha print. The hotel's restaurant is pure
Continental, from the classic garnishes to the creamy sauces. Two
rooms are set aside for travelers with disabilities. Children 12
and under stay for free. Panská 12, 111 21 Prague 1, tel. 02/2409–3111,
fax 02/2422–1240. 114 rooms, 10 suites. 2 restaurants, in-room safes,
minibars, 2 no-smoking floors, sauna. AE, DC, MC, V. www.hotel-palace.cz

$$$ AXA. Funky and functional, this 1932 high-rise was once a mainstay
of the budget-hotel crowd. Over the years, the rooms have certainly
improved; however, the lobby and public areas are still decidedly
tacky, with plastic flowers, lots of mirrors, and glaring lights.
There are scores of free weights in Axa's gym, making it one of
the best in Prague. Na Poříčí 40, 113 03 Prague 1, tel. 02/2481–2580,

fax 02/232–2172. 126 rooms, 6 suites. Restaurant, bar, pool, sauna, health club. AE, DC, MC, V. www.vol.cz/axa

$$$ CITY HOTEL MORAN. This renovated 19th-century town house has a bright, inviting lobby and equally bright and clean rooms that are modern, if slightly bland. Some upper-floor rooms have good views of Prague Castle. *Na Moráni 15, 120 00 Prague 2, tel. 02/2491–5208, fax 02/2492–0625. 57 rooms. Restaurant. AE, DC, MC, V.*

$$$ METEOR PLAZA. This Best Western hotel combines modern conveniences with historical ambience (Empress Maria Theresa's son, Joseph II, stayed here when he was passing through in the 18th century). The setting is ideal: a Baroque building that is only five minutes on foot from downtown. To get a sense of the hotel's age, visit the original 14th-century wine cellar. Rates drop markedly in midsummer and even more in winter. *Hybernská 6, 110 00 Prague 1, tel. 02/2419–2111, fax 02/2421–3005. 90 rooms, 6 suites. Restaurant, exercise room, parking (fee). AE, DC, MC, V. www.hotel-meteor.cz*

$$$ OPERA. Once the lodging of choice for divas performing at the nearby Státní opera (State Theater), the Opera greatly declined under the Communists. The mid-1990s saw the grand fin-de-siècle facade rejuvenated with a perky pink-and-white exterior paint job. This exuberance is strictly on the outside, though, and the room decor is modern and easy on the eyes. In the off-season a double room can be had for around 2,500 Kč. *Těšnov 13, 110 00 Prague 1, tel. 02/231–5609, fax 02/231–1477. 64 rooms. Restaurant, bar, minibars. AE, DC, MC, V.*

$$ HARMONY. This is one of the renovated, formerly state-owned standbys. A stern 1930s facade clashes with the bright, 1990s interior, but cheerful receptionists, comfortably casual rooms, and an easy 10-minute walk to the Old Town compensate for the aesthetic flaws. Ask for a room away from the bustle of one of Prague's busiest streets. *Na Poříčí 31, 110 00 Prague 1, tel. 02/232–0016, fax 02/231–0009. 60 rooms. 2 restaurants. AE, DC, MC, V.*

$$ SALVATOR. An efficiently run establishment just outside the Old Town, this pension offers more comforts than most in its class, including satellite TV and minibars in most rooms, and a combination breakfast room and bar with a billiard table. Rooms are pristine if plain, with the standard narrow beds; those without private bath also lack TVs but are a good value nonetheless. *Truhlářská 10, 110 00 Prague 1, tel. 02/231–2234, fax 02/231–6355. 28 rooms, 16 with bath, 7 suites. Breakfast room, parking (fee). AE (5% fee). Metro: Náměstí Republiky.*

SMÍCHOV

$$$ KINSKY GARDEN. You could walk the mile or so from this hotel to Prague Castle entirely on the tree-lined paths of Petřín, the hilly park that starts across the street. Opened in 1997, the hotel takes its name from a garden established by Count Rudolf Kinsky in 1825 on the southern side of Petřín. The public spaces and some rooms are not spacious, but everything is tasteful and comfortable. Try to get a room on one of the upper floors for a view of the park. The management and restaurant are Italian. *Holečkova 7, 150 00 Prague 5, tel. 02/5731–1173, fax 02/5731–1184. 60 rooms. Restaurant, bar, meeting room. AE, DC, MC, V.*

$$ MEPRO. Standard rooms and service and a reasonably central location make this small hotel worth considering. The Smíchov neighborhood offers a good range of restaurants (including the U Mikuláše Dačického wine tavern, across the street from the hotel) and nice strolls along the river or up the Petřín hill. *Viktora Huga 3, 150 00 Prague 5, tel. 02/548–549, fax 02/571–2380. 26 rooms. Snack bar. AE, MC, V.*

$$ PETR. Set in a quiet part of Smíchov, just a few minutes' stroll from the Lesser Quarter, this is an excellent value. As a "garni" hotel, it does not have a full-service restaurant, but it does serve breakfast (included in the price). The rooms are simply but adequately furnished. It's a 10-minute walk from metro Anděl (Line B).

Drtinova 17, 150 00 Prague 5, tel. 02/5731–4068, fax 02/5731–4072. 37 rooms, 2 suites. AE, MC, V.

$ BALKAN. Still holding its own as the city center's lone bare-bones budget hotel, the spartan Balkan is on a busy street not far from the Lesser Quarter and the Národní divadlo (National Theater). Breakfast is served for 85 Kč. *Svornosti 28, 150 00 Prague 5, tel./fax 02/5732–7180, 02/5732–2150, or 02/5732–5583. 24 rooms. Restaurant. AE (5% fee).*

ŽIŽKOV

$$ BERN. The cream-color Bern is a comfortable alternative to staying in the city center. Although rather far out, it is situated on several city bus routes into the New and Old Towns; buses run frequently even on evenings and weekends, and the trip takes 10–15 minutes. *Koněvova 28, 130 00 Prague 3, tel./fax 02/697–5807 or 02/697–4420. 26 rooms with shower. Restaurant, bar, air-conditioning, minibars. AE, DC, MC, V.*

$$ OLŠANKA. The main calling card of this boxy modern hotel is its outstanding 50-meter swimming pool and modern sports center, which includes a pair of tennis courts and aerobics classes. Rooms are clean and, though basic, have the most important hotel amenities. There's also a relaxing sauna with certain nights reserved for men, women, or both. (Note that the sports facilities may be closed in August.) The neighborhood is nondescript, but the Old Town is only 10 minutes away by direct tram. *Táboritská 23, 130 87 Prague 3, tel. 02/6709–2202, fax 02/2271–3315. 200 rooms. Restaurant, bar, pool, health club, meeting rooms. AE, MC, V.*

EASTERN SUBURBS

$$ ASTRA. The location best serves drivers coming into town from the east, although the nearby metro station makes this modern hotel easy to reach from the center. The neighborhood is quiet, if ordinary, and the rooms are more comfortable than most in this price range. *Mukařovská 1740/18, 100 00 Prague 10, tel. 02/781–3595, fax 02/781–0765. 43 rooms, 10 suites. Restaurant, nightclub. AE, DC, MC, V. Metro: Skalka (Line A), then walk south on Na padesátém about 5 mins to Mukařovská.*

$ APOLLO. This is a standard, no-frills, square-box hotel where clean rooms come at a fair price. Its primary flaw is its location: roughly 20 minutes away by metro and tram from the city center. *Kubišova 23, 182 00 Prague 8, tel. 02/688–0628, fax 02/688–4570. 35 rooms. MC, V. Metro: Nádraží Holešovice (Line C), then Tram 5, 14, or 17 to the Hercovka stop.*

$ PENSION LOUDA. ★ The friendly owners of this family-run guest house go out of their way to make you feel welcome. The large, spotless rooms are an exceptional bargain, and although the place is in the suburbs, the hilltop site offers a stunning view of greater Prague from the south-facing rooms. *Kubišova 10, 182 00 Prague 8, tel. 02/688–1491, fax 02/688–1488. 9 rooms. Sauna, exercise room. No credit cards. Metro: Nádraží Holešovice (Line C), then Tram 5, 14, or 17 to the Hercovka stop.*

WESTERN SUBURBS

$$$$ DIPLOMAT. This sprawling complex opened in 1990 and remains popular with business travelers thanks to its location between the airport and downtown. From the hotel, you can easily reach the city center by metro. The modern rooms may not exude much character, but they are tastefully furnished and quite comfortable. You can drive a miniature racing car at the indoor track next door. *Evropská 15, 160 00 Prague 6, tel. 02/2439–4111, fax 02/2439–4215. 369 rooms, 13 suites. 2 restaurants, bar, café, 2 no-smoking floors, sauna, exercise room, nightclub, meeting room, parking (fee). AE, DC, MC, V. Metro: Dejvická (Line A).*

$ PENZION SPRINT. Straightforward rooms, most of which have their own bathroom (however tiny), make the Sprint a fine choice. This pension is located on a quiet residential street, next to a large track and soccer field, in the outskirts of Prague about 20 minutes from the airport. Tram 18 rumbles directly to the Old Town from the Batérie stop just two blocks away. *Cukrovárnická 62, 160 00 Prague 6, tel. 02/312–3338, fax 02/312–1797. 21 rooms, 6 with bath. AE, MC, V.*

142

PRACTICAL INFORMATION

Air Travel

BOOKING

When you book **look for nonstop flights** and **remember that "direct" flights stop at least once.** Try to avoid connecting flights, which require a change of plane.

CARRIERS

ČSA (the Czech national carrier) offers direct flights all over the world to and from Ruzyně, including regular direct flights from New York to Prague (daily in high season) and flights from Montréal and Toronto to Prague two or three times a week.

Several other international airlines, including Delta, Lufthansa, SAS, KLM, and Air France, have good connections from cities in the United States and Canada to European bases and from there to Prague. British Airways and its budget line, Go, have daily nonstop service to Prague from London (with connections to major British cities). ČSA flies daily nonstop from London. Swissair flies daily via Zurich.

From New York, a nonstop flight to Prague takes eight hours; from the West Coast with a stopover, 14–16 hours. The flight from London takes around two hours.

➤ MAJOR AIRLINES: The following major airlines have offices in Prague: **Air Canada** (tel. 02/2489–2730); **Air France** (tel. 02/ 2422–7164); **Alitalia** (tel. 02/2419–4150); **American Airlines** (tel. 02/9623–6673); **British Airways** (tel. 02/2211–4444); **British Midland** (tel. 02/2481–0180); **ČSA** (tel. 02/2010–4310); **Delta** (tel. 02/2494–7332); **KLM** (tel. 02/2422–8678); **Lufthansa** (tel. 02/ 2481–1007); **SAS** (tel. 02/2481–1007); and **Swissair** (tel. 02/2481– 2111).

➤ FROM THE U.S.: ČSA (tel. 212/765–6022, tel. 02/2010–4310 in Prague).

CHECK-IN & BOARDING

Assuming that not everyone with a ticket will show up, airlines routinely overbook planes. When everyone does, airlines ask for volunteers to give up their seats. In return, these volunteers usually get a certificate for a free flight and are rebooked on the next flight out. If there are not enough volunteers, the airline must choose who will be denied boarding. The first to get bumped are passengers who checked in late and those flying on discounted tickets, so **get to the gate and check in as early as possible,** especially during peak periods.

Always **bring a government-issued photo I.D. to the airport.** You may be asked to show it before you are allowed to check in.

CUTTING COSTS

The least expensive airfares to Prague must usually be purchased in advance and are nonrefundable. It's smart to **call a number of airlines, and when you are quoted a good price, book it on the spot**—the same fare may not be available the next day. Always **check different routings** and look into using different airports. Travel agents, especially low-fare specialists, are helpful.

Consolidators are another good source. They buy tickets for scheduled international flights at reduced rates from the airlines, then sell them at prices that beat the best fare available directly from the airlines, usually without restrictions. Sometimes you can even get your money back if you need to return the ticket. Carefully read the fine print detailing penalties for changes and cancellations, and **confirm your consolidator reservation with the airline.**

➤ CONSOLIDATORS: **Cheap Tickets** (tel. 800/377–1000). **Discount Airline Ticket Service** (tel. 800/576–1600). **Unitravel** (tel. 800/325–2222). **Up & Away Travel** (tel. 212/889–2345). **World Travel Network** (tel. 800/409–6753).

ENJOYING THE FLIGHT

For more legroom, **request an emergency-aisle seat.** Don't sit in the row in front of the emergency aisle or in front of a bulkhead, where seats may not recline. If you have dietary concerns, **ask for special meals when booking.** These can be vegetarian, low-cholesterol, or kosher, for example. On long flights, try to maintain a normal routine, to help fight jet lag. At night, **get some sleep.** By day, **eat light meals, drink water** (not alcohol), and **move around the cabin** to stretch your legs.

HOW TO COMPLAIN

If your baggage goes astray or your flight goes awry, complain right away. Most carriers require that you **file a claim immediately.**

➤ AIRLINE COMPLAINTS: U.S. Department of Transportation **Aviation Consumer Protection Division** (C-75, Room 4107, Washington, DC 20590, tel. 202/366–2220, www.dot.gov/airconsumer). **Federal Aviation Administration Consumer Hotline** (tel. 800/322–7873).

Airport

Ruzyně Airport, 20 km (12 mi) northwest of the downtown area, is small but easily negotiated. Construction of a new terminal contiguous with the existing one has eased traffic flow.

➤ AIRPORT INFORMATION: **Ruzyně Airport** (tel. 02/2011–1111).

BETWEEN THE AIRPORT AND DOWNTOWN

The Cedqaz minibus shuttle links the airport with náměstí Republiky (Republic Square, just off the Old Town). It runs hourly, more often at peak periods, between 6 AM and 9:30 PM daily and makes an intermediate stop at the Dejvická metro station. The one-way fare is 90 Kč. The minibus also serves many hotels for 360 Kč, which is less than the taxi fare in most cases. Regular municipal bus service (Bus 119) connects the airport and the Dejvická station; the fare is 12 Kč (15 Kč if purchased from the driver), and the ticket is transferable to trams or the metro. From Dejvická you can take the metro to the city center. To reach Wenceslas Square, get off at the Mùstek station.

Taxis offer the easiest and most convenient way of getting downtown. The trip is a straight shot down Evropská Boulevard and takes approximately 20 minutes. The road is not usually busy, but anticipate an additional 20 minutes during rush hour (7 AM–9 AM and 3 PM–6 PM). The ride should cost 500 Kč–700 Kč.

Bus Travel

The Czech complex of regional bus lines known collectively as ČSAD operates its dense network from the sprawling Florenc station on Křižíkova (Metro: Florenc, Line B or C). This bus service is usually much quicker than the normal trains and more frequent than express trains, unless you're going to the major cities. Frequent bus service between Prague and Karlovy Vary makes the journey in only about two hours each way. Prices are quite low—essentially the same as those for second-class rail tickets. Buy your tickets from the ticket window at the bus station or directly from the driver on the bus. Buses can be full to bursting. On long-distance trips, it's a good idea to buy advance tickets when available (indicated by an R in a circle on timetables); get them at the local station or at some travel agencies. The only drawback to traveling by bus is figuring out the timetables. They are easy to read, but beware of the small letters denoting exceptions to the times given. If in doubt, inquire at the information window or ask someone for assistance.

Several bus companies run direct services between major Western European cities and Prague. Two with almost daily service from London are Kingscourt Express and Eurolines, both operating out of London's Victoria Coach Station. The trip takes about 20 hours and costs around $75 one-way.

For information about routes and schedules you can call the company, consult the confusingly displayed timetables posted at the station, or visit the information window in the lower level lobby, open daily from 6 AM to 9 PM. One of several Web sites with bus and train information in English is idos.datis.cdrail.cz.

➤ **BUS COMPANIES: ČSAD**: tel. 02/1034. **Kingscourt Express**: tel. 0181/673–7500 in London. **Eurolines**: tel. 0171/730–3466 in London.

Business Hours

Though hours vary, most banks are open weekdays 8–5. Private exchange offices usually have longer hours. Museums are usually open daily except Monday 9–5 or 10–6; they tend to stop selling tickets an hour before closing time. Stores are open weekdays 9–6. Some grocery stores open at 6 AM. Department stores often stay open until 7 PM.

Car Rental

Major rental agencies are represented throughout the region, but **don't overlook local firms;** they can offer bargains, but watch for hidden insurance conditions. Rates and regulations vary widely from country to country.

There are no special requirements for renting a car in the Czech Republic, but be sure to shop around, as prices can differ greatly. Avis, Hertz, and other major firms offer Western makes starting at around $45 per day or $300 per week, which includes insurance, damage waiver, and VAT; cars equipped with automatic transmission and air-conditioning are available, but it's best to reserve well in advance if you have special needs—try calling the firm's U.S. reservation number before you leave home. It may be less expensive to reserve from home as well. Smaller local companies, on the other hand, can rent Czech cars for significantly less, but the service and insurance coverage may be inferior. A surcharge of 5%–12% applies to rental cars picked up at Prague's Ruzyně Airport.

MAJOR AGENCIES IN PRAGUE: **Alamo** (Hilton Hotel, tel. 02/2484–2407, or Ruzyně Airport, tel. 02/2011–3676). **Avis** (Klimentská 46 and Ruzyně Airport, tel. 02/2185–1225). **Budget** (Hotel Inter-Continental, nám. Curieových 5, tel. 02/231–9595, or Ruzyně Airport, tel. 02/2011–3253). **Hertz** (Karlovo nám. 28, tel. 02/2223–1010, or Ruzyně Airport, tel. 02/312–0717). **Thrifty** (Washingtonova 9, tel. 02/2421–1587, or Ruzyně Airport, tel. 02/2011–4370).

CUTTING COSTS

To get the best deal, **book through a travel agent who will shop around.** Do **look into wholesalers,** companies that do not own fleets but rent in bulk from those that do and often offer better rates than traditional car-rental operations. Payment must be made before you leave home.

➤ WHOLESALERS: **Auto Europe** (tel. 207/842–2000 or 800/223–5555, fax 800/235–6321, www.autoeurope.com). **DER Travel Services** (9501 W. Devon Ave., Rosemont, IL 60018, tel. 800/782–2424, fax 800/282–7474 for information; 800/860–9944 for brochures, www.dertravel.com). **Kemwel Holiday Autos** (tel. 800/678–0678, fax 914/825–3160, www.kemwel.com).

INSURANCE

When driving a rented car you are generally responsible for any damage to or loss of the vehicle. Before you rent see what coverage your personal auto-insurance policy and credit cards already provide.

Before you buy collision coverage, check your existing policies—you may already be covered. However, collision policies that car-rental companies sell for European rentals usually do not include stolen-vehicle coverage.

REQUIREMENTS & RESTRICTIONS

A permit is required to drive on expressways and other four-lane highways. They cost 100 Kč for 10 days, 200 Kč for one month, and 800 Kč for one year, and are sold at border crossings, some service stations, and all post offices. If you intend to drive across a border, ask about **restrictions on driving into other countries.** The minimum age required for renting is usually 21 or older, and some companies also have maximum ages; be sure to inquire when making your arrangements.

SURCHARGES

Before you pick up a car in one city and leave it in another, **ask about drop-off charges or one-way service fees,** which can be substantial. Note, too, that some rental agencies charge extra if you return the car before the time specified in your contract. To avoid a hefty refueling fee, **fill the tank just before you turn in the car,** but be aware that gas stations near the rental outlet may overcharge.

Car Travel

Traveling by car is the easiest and most flexible way of seeing the Czech Republic—other than Prague. If you intend to visit only the capital, you can do without a car. The city center is congested and difficult to navigate, with stop-and-go traffic during the day, and you'll save yourself a lot of hassle by sticking to public transportation.

Should you decide to drive anyway, pay particular attention to the trams, which have the right-of-way in every situation. Avoid, if you can, driving in the congested and labyrinthine Old Town. If driving in from outside the city, simply follow the signs to CENTRUM (city center). Prague is well served by major roads and highways from anywhere in the country; you can take the E48 directly from Prague to Karlovy Vary.

The most convenient ferry ports for Prague are Hoek van Holland and Ostend. To reach Prague from either ferry port, drive first to Cologne (Köln) and then through either Dresden or Frankfurt.

In case of an accident or breakdown, *see* Emergency Services, *below.*

PARKING

Parking is permitted in the center of Prague on a growing number of streets with parking meters or in the few small lots within walking distance of the historic center—but parking spaces are scarce. A meter with a green stripe lets you park up to six hours; an orange-stripe meter gives you two. (Use change in the meters.) A sign with a blue circle outlined in red with a diagonal red slash indicates a no-parking zone. Avoid the blue-marked spaces, which are reserved for local residents. Violaters may find a "boot" immobilizing their vehicle.

There's an underground lot at náměstí Jana Palacha, near Old Town Square. There are also park-and-ride (P+R) lots at some suburban metro stations, including Skalka (Line A), Zličín and Černý Most (Line B), and Nádraží Holešovice and Opatov (Line C).

ROAD CONDITIONS

The Prague city center is mostly a snarl of traffic, one-way streets, and tram lines. If you plan to drive outside the capital, there are few four-lane highways, but most of the roads are in reasonably good shape, and traffic is usually light. Roads can be poorly marked, however, so before you start out, buy one of the inexpensive multilingual auto atlases available at any bookstore.

RULES OF THE ROAD

Throughout the Czech Republic, driving is on the right and the same basic rules of the road practiced in the the United States and the rest of Europe apply. A right turn on red is permitted only when indicated by a green arrow. Signposts with yellow diamonds indicate a main road where drivers have the right of way. The speed limit is 130 kph (78 mph) on four-lane highways, 90 kph (56 mph) on open roads, and 50 kph (30 mph) in built-up areas. Seat belts are compulsory, and drinking before driving is absolutely prohibited. Passengers under 12 years of age, or less than 150 cm (5 ft) in height, must ride in the back seat.

A word of caution: If you have any alcohol whatsoever in your body, do not drive. Penalties are fierce, and the blood-alcohol limit is practically zero.

AUTO CLUBS

➤ IN PRAGUE: **Autoturist** (Prague 4, Na Strži 9, tel. 02/6110–4333).

➤ IN AUSTRALIA: **Australian Automobile Association** (tel. 02/6247–7311).

➤ IN CANADA: **Canadian Automobile Association** (CAA, tel. 613/247–0117).

➤ IN NEW ZEALAND: **New Zealand Automobile Association** (tel. 09/377–4660).

➤ IN THE U.K.: **Automobile Association** (AA, tel. 0990/500–600). **Royal Automobile Club** (RAC, tel. 0990/722–722 for membership; 0345/121–345 for insurance).

➤ IN THE U.S.: **American Automobile Association** (tel. 800/564–6222).

EMERGENCY SERVICES

In case of a breakdown, your best friend is the telephone. Try contacting your **rental agency** or ABA or ÚAMK.

➤ EMERGENCY CONTACTS: **ABA** (tel. 124, or 0124 in rural areas). **ÚAMK** (tel. 123, or 0123 in rural areas).

GASOLINE

Gas stations are easy to come by on major thoroughfares and in Prague. Many are open around the clock. At least two grades of gasoline are sold, usually 90–93 octane (regular) and 94–98 octane (super). Lead-free gasoline is now available in most gas stations.

ROAD MAPS

The ubiquitous 24-hour gas stations often sell road maps, or try a bookstore. In Prague, the downstairs level of the Jan

Kanzelsberger bookshop on Wenceslas Square has a good selection of hiking maps and auto atlases.

➤ **Road Maps: Jan Kanzelsberger** (Václavské nám. 42, tel. 02/2421–7335).

Children in Prague

LODGING
Most hotels in Prague allow children under a certain age to stay in their parents' room at no extra charge, but others charge for them as extra adults; be sure to **find out the cutoff age for children's discounts.** Some spa hotels don't allow children under 12. Young visitors to the Czech Republic will enjoy staying at one of Prague's picturesque floating "botels." For further information contact the Czech Tourist Authority (☞ Visitor Information, *below*). Prague's luxurious Palace and Savoy hotels, managed by Vienna International, allow children under 12 to stay free in their parents' room.

SIGHTS & ATTRACTIONS
Places that are especially appealing to children are indicated by a rubber duckie icon in the margins throughout the book.

TRANSPORTATION
In the Czech Republic, car passengers under 12 years of age, or less than 150 cm (5 ft) in height, must ride in the back seat.

Customs & Duties

When shopping, **keep receipts** for all purchases. Upon reentering the country, **be ready to show customs officials what you've bought.** If you feel a duty is incorrect or object to the way your clearance was handled, note the inspector's badge number and ask to see a supervisor. If the problem isn't resolved, write to the appropriate authorities, beginning with the port director at your point of entry.

IN THE CZECH REPUBLIC

You may import duty-free into the Czech Republic tobacco products equivalent to 200 cigarettes, 100 cigarillos, 250 grams of tobacco, or 50 cigars; 1 liter of spirits, 2 liters of wine, and personal medicines, as well as gifts and personal items valued at up to 6,000 Kč (3,000 Kč for visitors under 15) (about $170/$85). If you are bringing into the country any valuables or foreign-made equipment from home, such as cameras, it's wise to carry the original receipts with you or register the items with U.S. Customs before you leave (Form 4457). Otherwise you could end up paying duty upon your return.

IN AUSTRALIA

Australian residents who are 18 or older may bring home $A400 worth of souvenirs and gifts (including jewelry), 250 cigarettes or 250 grams of tobacco, and 1,125 ml of alcohol (including wine, beer, and spirits). Residents under 18 may bring back $A200 worth of goods. Prohibited items include meat products. Seeds, plants, and fruits need to be declared upon arrival.

➤ INFORMATION: **Australian Customs Service** (Regional Director, Box 8, Sydney, NSW 2001, Australia, tel. 02/9213–2000, fax 02/9213–4000, www.customs.gov.au).

IN CANADA

Canadian residents who have been out of Canada for at least 7 days may bring home C$500 worth of goods duty-free. If you've been away less than 7 days but more than 48 hours, the duty-free allowance drops to C$200; if your trip lasts 24–48 hours, the allowance is C$50. You may not pool allowances with family members. Goods claimed under the C$500 exemption may follow you by mail; those claimed under the lesser exemptions must accompany you. Alcohol and tobacco products may be included in the 7-day and 48-hour exemptions but not in the 24-hour exemption. If you meet the age requirements of the province or territory through which you reenter Canada, you may bring in, duty-free, 1.14 liters (40 imperial ounces) of wine or liquor or 24 12-ounce cans or bottles of beer or ale. If you are 16 or older you may bring in, duty-free, 200 cigarettes and 50 cigars. Check ahead of time with Revenue Canada or the Department of Agriculture for policies regarding meat products, seeds, plants, and fruits.

You may send an unlimited number of gifts worth up to C$60 each duty-free to Canada. Label the package UNSOLICITED GIFT—VALUE UNDER $60. Alcohol and tobacco are excluded.

➤ INFORMATION: **Revenue Canada** (2265 St. Laurent Blvd. S, Ottawa, Ontario K1G 4K3, Canada, tel. 613/993–0534; 800/461–9999 in Canada, fax 613/991–4126, www.ccra-adrc.gc.ca).

IN NEW ZEALAND
Homeward-bound residents 17 or older may bring back $700 worth of souvenirs and gifts. Your duty-free allowance also includes 4.5 liters of wine or beer; one 1,125-ml bottle of spirits; and either 200 cigarettes, 250 grams of tobacco, 50 cigars, or a combination of the three up to 250 grams. Prohibited items include meat products, seeds, plants, and fruits.

➤ INFORMATION: **New Zealand Customs** (Custom House, 50 Anzac Ave., Box 29, Auckland, New Zealand, tel. 09/300–5399, fax 09/359–6730), www.customs.govt.nz.

IN THE U.K.
From countries outside the EU, including the Czech Republic, you may bring home, duty-free, 200 cigarettes or 50 cigars; 1 liter of spirits or 2 liters of fortified or sparkling wine or liqueurs; 2 liters of still table wine; 60 ml of perfume; 250 ml of toilet water; plus £136 worth of other goods, including gifts and souvenirs. If returning from outside the EU, prohibited items include meat products, seeds, plants, and fruits.

➤ INFORMATION: **HM Customs and Excise** (Dorset House, Stamford St., Bromley, Kent BR1 1XX, U.K., tel. 020/7202–4227, www.hmce.gov.uk).

IN THE U.S.

U.S. residents who have been out of the country for at least 48 hours (and who have not used the $400 allowance or any part of it in the past 30 days) may bring home $400 worth of foreign goods duty-free.

U.S. residents 21 and older may bring back 1 liter of alcohol duty-free. In addition, regardless of your age, you are allowed 200 cigarettes and 100 non-Cuban cigars. Antiques, which the U.S. Customs Service defines as objects more than 100 years old, enter duty-free, as do original works of art done entirely by hand, including paintings, drawings, and sculptures.

You may also mail or ship packages home duty-free: up to $200 worth of goods for personal use, with a limit of one parcel per addressee per day (except alcohol or tobacco products or perfume worth more than $5); label the package PERSONAL USE and attach a list of its contents and their retail value. Do not label the package UNSOLICITED GIFT or your duty-free exemption will drop to $100. Mailed items do not affect your duty-free allowance on your return.

➤ INFORMATION: **U.S. Customs Service** (1300 Pennsylvania Ave. NW, Washington, DC 20229, www.customs.gov; inquiries tel. 202/354–1000; complaints c/o 1300 Pennsylvania Ave. NW, Room 5.4D, Washington, DC 20229; registration of equipment c/o Resource Management, tel. 202/354–1000).

Dining

The restaurants we list are the cream of the crop in each price category. Unless otherwise noted, the restaurants listed are open daily for lunch and dinner.

RESERVATIONS & DRESS

Reservations are always a good idea: we mention them only when they're essential or not accepted. Book as far ahead as you can, and reconfirm as soon as you arrive. We mention dress only when men are required to wear a jacket or a jacket and tie.

Disabilities & Accessibility

Provisions for travelers with disabilities in Prague are extremely limited; probably the best solution is to travel with a nondisabled companion. While many hotels, especially large American or international chains, offer some wheelchair-accessible rooms, special facilities at museums and restaurants and on public transportation are difficult to find.

➤ LOCAL RESOURCES: **Sdružení zdravotné postižených** (Association of Disabled Persons; Karlínské nám. 12, Prague 8, tel. 02/2481–5914, www.czechia.com/szdp).

LODGING

Most hotels take few or no measures to accommodate travelers with disabilities. Your best bets the best are newer hotels and international chains.

RESERVATIONS

When discussing accessibility with an operator or reservations agent, **ask hard questions.** Are there any stairs, inside *or* out? Are there grab bars next to the toilet *and* in the shower/tub? How wide is the doorway to the room? To the bathroom?

SIGHTS & ATTRACTIONS

Most tourist attractions in the region pose significant problems. Many are historic structures without ramps or other means to improve accessibility. Streets are often cobblestone, and potholes are common.

TRANSPORTATION

A few Czech trains are equipped with carriages for travelers using wheelchairs. Some stations on the Prague metro have elevators, and there are two lines of accessible buses, but the system is light-years from being barrier-free.

➤ COMPLAINTS: **Disability Rights Section** (U.S. Department of Justice, Civil Rights Division, Box 66738, Washington, DC 20035-6738, tel. 202/514–0301 or 800/514–0301; 202/514–0383 TTY;

800/514–0383 TTY, fax 202/307–1198, www.usdoj.gov/crt/ada/adahom1.htm) for general complaints. **Aviation Consumer Protection Division** (☞ Air Travel, *above*) for airline-related problems. **Civil Rights Office** (U.S. Department of Transportation, Departmental Office of Civil Rights, S-30, 400 7th St. SW, Room 10215, Washington, DC 20590, tel. 202/366–4648, fax 202/366–9371) for problems with surface transportation.

➤ INFORMATION: **Prague public transport** (tel. 02/2264–6055).

Electricity

To use your U.S.-purchased electric-powered equipment, **bring a converter and adapter.** The electrical current in the Czech Republic is 220 volts, 50 cycles alternating current (AC); wall outlets generally take plugs with two round prongs.

If your appliances are dual-voltage, you'll need only an adapter. Don't use 110-volt outlets marked FOR SHAVERS ONLY for high-wattage appliances such as blow-dryers. Most laptops operate equally well on 110 and 220 volts and so require only an adapter.

Emergencies

➤ EMBASSIES: **Canadian Embassy** (Mickiewiczova 6, Hradčany, tel. 02/7210–1800). **U.K. Embassy** (Thunovská 14, Lesser Quarter, tel. 02/5753–0278). **U.S. Embassy** (Tržiště 15, Lesser Quarter, tel. 02/5753–0663).

➤ GENERAL EMERGENCY CONTACTS: **Federal Police** (tel. 158). **Prague city police** (156). **Western Bohemia Police** (tel. 158). **Ambulance** (tel. 155).

➤ LOST CREDIT CARDS: **American Express** (tel. 02/2421–9978); **Diners Club** (tel. 02/6731–4485); **Visa** (tel. 02/2412–5353); **MasterCard** (tel. 02/2424–8110).

➤ MEDICAL EMERGENCIES: **Lékařská služba první pomoci** (district first-aid clinic; Downtown: Palackého 5, tel. 02/2494–9181); **Na**

Homolce Hospital (Roentgenova 2, Prague 5, tel. 02/5727–2146 weekdays [foreigners' department]; 02/5721–1111; 02/5727–2191); **First Medical Clinic of Prague** (Tylovo nám. 3/15, Prague 2, tel. 02/2425–1319); **American Medical Center** (Janovského 48, Prague 7, tel. 02/807–756 for 24 hr service). Be prepared to pay in cash for medical treatment, whether you are insured or not. **Dentist** (Palackého 5, tel. 02/2494–6981 for 24-hr emergency service).

➤ PHARMACIES: **Lékárna U Anděla** (Štefánikova 6, Prague 5, tel. 02/537–039 or 02/5732–0918). **Lékárna** (Belgická 37, Prague 2, tel. 02/2251–9731).

Gay & Lesbian Travel

Prague fosters a growing gay and lesbian scene, but up-to-date information is not easy to find. You could try visiting one of the gathering places that attract both gays and straights, such as the Radost FX club.

➤ GAY- & LESBIAN-FRIENDLY TRAVEL AGENCIES: **Different Roads Travel** (8383 Wilshire Blvd., Suite 902, Beverly Hills, CA 90211, tel. 323/651–5557 or 800/429–8747, fax 323/651–3678). **Kennedy Travel** (314 Jericho Turnpike, Floral Park, NY 11001, tel. 516/352–4888 or 800/237–7433, fax 516/354–8849, www.kennedytravel.com). **Now Voyager** (4406 18th St., San Francisco, CA 94114, tel. 415/626–1169 or 800/255–6951, fax 415/626–8626, www.nowvoyager.com). **Skylink Travel and Tour** (1006 Mendocino Ave., Santa Rosa, CA 95401, tel. 707/546–9888 or 800/225–5759, fax 707/546–9891, www.skylinktravel.com), serving lesbian travelers.

Getting Around

To see Prague properly, there is no alternative to walking. And the walking couldn't be more pleasant—most of it along the beautiful bridges and cobblestone streets of the city's historic core. Before venturing out, however, be sure you have a good map. The city is divided into 10 administrative districts; Prague 1 and part of Prague 2 lie entirely within the historic center, and the castle area is bordered by Prague 6 and Prague 7.

Navigation is relatively simple once you know the basic street sign words: *ulice* (street, abbreviated to ul., commonly dropped in printed addresses); *náměstí* (square, abbreviated to nám.); and *třída* (avenue). As in most Czech towns, each building in Prague has two numbers, a confusing practice with historic roots. In Prague, the blue tags mark the street address (usually).

BY BUS AND TRAM

Prague's extensive bus and streetcar network allows for fast, efficient travel throughout the city. Tickets are the same as those used for the metro, although you validate them at machines inside the bus or tram. Tickets (*jízdenky*) can be bought at hotels, some newsstands, and from dispensing machines in the metro stations. The basic, transferable ticket costs 12 Kč. It permits one hour's travel throughout the metro, tram, and bus network between 5 AM and 8 PM on weekdays, or 90 minutes' travel at other times. Single-ride tickets cost 8 Kč and allow one 15-minute ride on a tram or bus, without transfer, or a metro journey of up to four stations lasting less than 30 minutes (transfer between lines is allowed). You can also buy a one-day pass allowing unlimited use of the system for 70 Kč, a three-day pass for 180 Kč, a seven-day pass for 250 Kč, or a 15-day pass for 280 Kč. The passes can be purchased at the main metro stations, from ticket machines, and at some newsstands in the center. A pass is not valid until stamped in the orange machines in metro stations or aboard trams *and* the required information is entered on the back (there are instructions in English). A refurbished old tram, No. 91, travels through the Old Town and Lesser Quarter on summer weekends. The metro shuts down at midnight, but Trams 50–59 and Buses 500 and above run all night. Night trams run at 40-minute intervals, and all routes intersect at the corner of Lazarská and Spálená streets in the New Town near the Národní třída metro station.

BY SUBWAY

Prague's subway system, the metro, is clean and reliable; the stations are marked with an inconspicuous M sign. Trains run daily from 5 AM to midnight. Validate your ticket at an orange machine before descending the escalator. Trains are patrolled often; the fine for riding without a valid ticket is 200 Kč. Beware of pickpockets, who often operate in large groups on crowded trams and metro cars.

BY TAXI

Dishonest taxi drivers are the shame of the nation. Luckily you probably won't need to rely on taxis for trips within the city center (it's usually easier to walk or take the subway). Typical scams include drivers doctoring the meter or simply failing to turn the meter on and then demanding an exorbitant sum at the end of the ride. In an honest cab, the meter starts at 25 Kč and increases by 17 Kč per km (½ mi) or 4 Kč per minute at rest. (The Airport Cars taxis operating from, but not to, the airport have a monopoly and charge slightly higher rates.) Most rides within town should cost no more than 80 Kč–150 Kč. To minimize the chances of getting ripped off, avoid taxi stands in Wenceslas Square, Old Town Square, and other heavily touristed areas. The best alternative is to phone for a taxi in advance. Many firms have English-speaking operators.

➤ REPUTABLE TAXI COMPANIES: **AAA Taxi** (tel. 02/1080). **Profitaxi** (tel. 02/1035).

GUIDED TOURS

Čedok (☞ Visitor Information, *below*) offers a three-and-a-half-hour "Grand City Tour," a combination bus and walking venture that covers all the major sights with commentary in English. It departs daily at 9:30 AM year-round, and also at 2 PM from April through October, from opposite the Prašná brána (Powder Tower) on Republic Square, near the main Čedok office. The price is about 750 Kč. "Historic Prague on Foot" is a slower-paced, three-hour walking tour for 400 Kč. From April through

October, it departs Republic Square on Wednesday, Friday, and Sunday at 9:30 AM; in the off-season, it departs Friday at 9:30 AM. More tours are offered, especially in summer, and the schedules may well vary according to demand. You can also contact Čedok's main office to arrange a personalized walking tour. Times and itineraries are negotiable; prices start at around 500 Kč per hour.

Very similar tours by other operators also depart daily from Republic Square, Národní třída near Jungmannovo náměstí, and Wenceslas Square. Prices are generally a couple hundred crowns less than for Čedok's tours. Themed walking tours are very popular as well. You can choose medieval architecture, "Velvet Revolution walks," visits to Communist monuments, and any number of pub crawls. Each year, four or five small operators do these tours, which generally last a couple of hours and cost 200 Kč–300 Kč. Inquire at Prague Information Service (☞ Visitor Information, *below*) or a major ticket agency for the current season's offerings.

Most of Prague's tour operators offer excursions to Karlovy Vary; inquire at the Prague Information Service or American Express. Čedok offers one-day and longer tours covering western Bohemia's major sights, as well as curative vacations at many Czech spas.

Holidays

January 1; Easter Monday; May 1 (Labor Day); May 8 (Liberation Day); July 5 (Sts. Cyril and Methodius); July 6 (Jan Hus); October 28 (Czech National Day); and December 24, 25, and 26.

Language

Czech, a Slavic language closely related to Slovak and Polish, is the official language of the Czech Republic. Learning English is popular among young people, but German is still the most useful language for tourists, especially outside Prague.

Lodging

The lodgings we list are the cream of the crop in each price category. We always list the facilities that are available—but we don't specify whether they cost extra: when pricing accommodations, always ask what's included.

B&B RESERVATION AGENCIES

Most local information offices also book rooms in hotels, pensions, and private accommodations. Do-it-yourself travelers should keep a sharp eye out for room-for-rent signs reading ZIMMER FREI, PRIVAT, or UBYTOVÁNÍ.

➤ HOME-STAY RESERVATIONS: **Czechbook Agency** (Jopes Mill, Trebrownbridge, near Liskeard, Cornwall PL14 3PX, tel./fax 01503/240629).

HOSTELS

No matter what your age you can **save on lodging costs by staying at hostels.** In some 5,000 locations in more than 70 countries around the world, Hostelling International (HI),the umbrella group for a number of national youth-hostel associations, offers single-sex, dorm-style beds and, at many hostels, couples rooms and family accommodations. Membership in any HI national hostel association, open to travelers of all ages, allows you to stay in HI-affiliated hostels at member rates (one-year membership is about $25 for adults; hostels run about $10–$25 per night). Members also have priority if the hostel is full; they're eligible for discounts around the world, even on rail and bus travel in some countries. Czech hostels tend to be either backpacker-happy, party-all-night places, or affiliated with sports clubs or colleges. Most accommodation services in Prague book hostel rooms.

➤ LOCAL HOSTEL: **Travellers' Hostel** (Dlouhá 33, tel. 02/231–1318).

Organizations: Hostelling International—American Youth Hostels (733 15th St. NW, Suite 840, Washington, DC 20005, tel.

202/783–6161, fax 202/783–6171, www.hiayh.org). **Hostelling International—Canada** (400–205 Catherine St., Ottawa, Ontario K2P 1C3, Canada, tel. 613/237–7884, fax 613/237–7868, www.hostellingintl.ca). **KMC Travel Service** (Karolíny Světlé 30, tel. 02/2222–1328). **Youth Hostel Association of England and Wales** (Trevelyan House, 8 St. Stephen's Hill, St. Albans, Hertfordshire AL1 2DY, U.K., tel. 0870/8708808, fax 01727/844126, www.yha.org.uk). **Australian Youth Hostel Association** (10 Mallett St., Camperdown, NSW 2050, Australia, tel. 02/9565–1699, fax 02/9565–1325, www.yha.com.au). **Youth Hostels Association of New Zealand** (Box 436, Christchurch, New Zealand, tel. 03/379–9970, fax 03/365–4476, www.yha.org.nz).

HOTELS

Throughout the past decade the quality of hotels in Prague improved notably. Many formerly state-run hotels were privatized, much to their benefit—a transition process that is still on-going in some countries. International hotel chains have established a strong presence in the region; while they may not be strong on local character, they do provide a reliably high standard of quality. Hotels listed throughout the book have private bath unless otherwise noted.

➤ Toll-Free Numbers: **Marriott** (tel. 800/228–9290, www. marriott.com). **Radisson** (tel. 800/333–3333, www.radisson.com).

Mail & Shipping

POSTAL RATES

In 2000, postcards to the United States and Canada cost 8 Kč; letters up to 20 grams in weight, 13 Kč. Postcards to Great Britain cost 7 Kč; letters, 9 Kč. You can buy stamps at post offices, hotels, and shops that sell postcards.

RECEIVING MAIL

If you don't know where you'll be staying, American Express mail service is a great convenience, available at no charge to anyone holding an American Express credit card or carrying American

Express traveler's checks. The American Express office (*see* Travel Agencies, *below*) is on Wenceslas Square in central Prague. You can also have mail held *poste restante* (general delivery) at post offices in major towns, but the letters should be marked Pošta 1, to designate the city's main post office. The poste restante window in Prague is at the main post office. You will be asked for identification when you collect your mail.

➤ Post Office: **Main post office** (Jindřišská ul. 14).

Money Matters

Prices throughout this guide are given for adults. Substantially reduced fees are almost always available for children, students, and senior citizens.

ATMS

ATMs are common in Prague and more often than not are part of the Cirrus and Plus networks.

COSTS

With inflation down to manageable levels, the Czech Republic is still generally a bargain by Western standards. Prague remains the exception. Hotel prices in particular are often higher than the facilities would warrant. Nevertheless, you can still find bargain private accommodations. The prices at tourist resorts outside the capital are lower and, in the outlying areas and off the beaten track, very low. It is an unfortunate fact that many venues such as museums, castles, and certain clubs charge a higher entrance fee for foreigners than they charge for Czechs. A few hotels still follow this practice too. Venue staff can be quite militant about defending this policy, which is legally acceptable in the Czech Republic, and protesting such discrimination when it happens will usually get you nowhere.

CREDIT CARDS

Credit cards are accepted in places that cater regularly to foreign tourists and business travelers: hotels, restaurants, and shops, particularly in major urban centers. When you leave the beaten path, be prepared to pay cash. Always inquire about credit card policies when booking hotel rooms. Visa and EuroCard/MasterCard are the most commonly accepted credit cards in the region.

It's smart to **write down (and keep separate) the number of each credit card you're carrying** along with the international service phone number that usually appears on the card.

Throughout this guide, the following abbreviations are used: **AE,** American Express; **D,** Discover; **DC,** Diners Club; **MC,** Master Card; and **V,** Visa.

CURRENCY

The unit of currency in the Czech Republic is the koruna, or crown (Kč), which is divided into 100 haléřů, or hellers. There are (little-used) coins of 10, 20, and 50 hellers; coins of 1, 2, 5, 10, 20, and (rarely) 50 Kč; and notes of 50, 100, 200, 500, 1,000, 2,000, and 5,000 Kč. Notes of 1,000 Kč and up may not always be accepted for small purchases.

CURRENCY EXCHANGE

Try to **avoid exchanging money at hotels or private exchange booths,** including the ubiquitous Chequepoint and Exact Change booths. They routinely take commissions of 8%–10%. The best places to exchange are at bank counters, where the commissions average 1%–3%, or at ATMs. The koruna is fully convertible, which means it can be purchased outside the country and exchanged into other currencies. Although fees charged for ATM transactions may be higher abroad than at home, Cirrus and Plus exchange rates are excellent, because they are based on wholesale rates offered only by major banks. You often won't do as well at exchange booths in airports or rail and bus stations, in hotels, in restaurants, or in stores, although you may find their hours more convenient. To avoid lines at airport exchange booths, **get a bit of local currency before you leave home.**

At press time the exchange rate was around 35 Kč to the U.S. dollar, 24 Kč to the Canadian dollar, and 56 Kč to the pound sterling.

➤ EXCHANGE SERVICES: **International Currency Express** (tel. 888/278–6628 for orders, www.foreignmoney.com). **Thomas Cook Currency Services** (tel. 800/287–7362 for telephone orders and retail locations, www.us.thomascook.com).

SAMPLE PRICES

A cup of coffee, about 30 Kč; public museum or castle entrance, 20 Kč–150 Kč; private museum entrance, up to 450 Kč; a good theater seat, up to 500 Kč; a cinema seat, 60 Kč–100 Kč; ½ liter (pint) of Czech beer, 15 Kč–50 Kč; a 2 km (1 mi) taxi ride, 60 Kč–200 Kč; a bottle of Moravian wine in a good restaurant, 140 Kč–400 Kč; a glass (2 deciliters or 7 ounces) of wine, 35 Kč–60 Kč.

Packing

Western dress of virtually any kind is considered stylish: A sports jacket for men and a dress or pants for women are appropriate for an evening out. Everywhere else, you'll feel comfortable in casual pants or jeans. Take a pair of sturdy walking shoes and be prepared to use them. High heels will present considerable problems on the cobblestone streets of Prague.

In your carry-on luggage, **pack an extra pair of eyeglasses or contact lenses** and **enough of any medication you take** to last the entire trip. You may also ask your doctor to write a spare prescription using the drug's generic name, since brand names may vary from country to country. In luggage to be checked, **never pack prescription drugs or valuables.** To avoid customs delays, carry medications in their original packaging. And don't forget to carry with you the addresses of offices that handle refunds of lost traveler's checks.

CHECKING LUGGAGE

How many carry-on bags you can bring with you is up to the airline. Most allow two, but not always, so make sure that everything you carry aboard will fit under your seat or in the overhead bin, and get to the gate early. Note that if you have a seat at the back of the plane, you'll probably board first, while the overhead bins are still empty.

When flying internationally, note that baggage allowances may be determined not by piece but by weight—generally 88 pounds (40 kilograms) in first class, 66 pounds (30 kilograms) in business class, and 44 pounds (20 kilograms) in economy.

Airline liability for baggage is limited to $1,250 per person on flights within the United States. On international flights it amounts to $9.07 per pound or $20 per kilogram for checked baggage (roughly $640 per 70-pound bag) and $400 per passenger for unchecked baggage. You can buy additional coverage at check-in for about $10 per $1,000 of coverage, but it excludes a list of items, shown on your airline ticket.

Before departure, **itemize your bags' contents** and their worth, and label the bags with your name, address, and phone number. (If you use your home address, cover it so potential thieves can't see it readily.) Inside each bag, **pack a copy of your itinerary.** At check-in, **make sure that each bag is correctly tagged** with the destination airport's three-letter code. If your bags arrive damaged or fail to arrive at all, file a written report with the airline before leaving the airport.

Passports & Visas

U.S., Canadian, and British citizens need only a valid passport to visit the Czech Republic as tourists. U.S. citizens may stay for 30 days without a visa; British and Canadian citizens, six months. A new law effective Jan. 1, 2000, may raise additional bureaucratic obstacles in the path of those wishing to stay longer. Those interested in working or living in the Czech Republic are advised to contact the Czech embassy or consulate in their home country well in advance of their trip.

When traveling internationally, **carry your passport** even if you don't need one (it's always the best form of ID) and **make two photocopies of the data page** (one for someone at home and another for you, carried separately from your passport). If you lose your passport, promptly call the nearest embassy or consulate and the local police.

PASSPORT OFFICES

The best time to apply for a passport or to renew is in fall and winter. Before any trip, check your passport's expiration date, and, if necessary, renew it as soon as possible.

➤ **AUSTRALIAN CITIZENS: Australian Passport Office** (tel. 131–232, www.dfat.gov.au/passports).

➤ **CANADIAN CITIZENS: Passport Office** (tel. 819/994–3500; 800/567–6868 in Canada, www.dfait-maeci.gc.ca/passport).

➤ **NEW ZEALAND CITIZENS: New Zealand Passport Office** (tel. 04/494–0700, www.passports.govt.nz).

➤ **U.K. CITIZENS: London Passport Office** (tel. 0870/521–0410, www.ukpa.gov.uk) for fees and documentation requirements and to request an emergency passport.

➤ **U.S. CITIZENS: National Passport Information Center** (tel. 900/225–5674; calls are 35¢ per minute for automated service, $1.05 per minute for operator service; www.travel.state.gov/npicinfo.html).

Rest Rooms

Public rest rooms are more common, and cleaner, than they used to be in the Czech Republic. You nearly always have to pay 2 Kč–10 Kč to the attendant. Restaurant and bar toilets are generally for customers only, but, as prices are low, this isn't a significant burden.

Safety

In the Czech Republic, except for widely scattered attacks against people of color, violent crime against tourists is extremely rare. Pickpocketing and bill-padding are the most common complaints.

LOCAL SCAMS

To avoid potential trouble: Ask taxi drivers what the approximate fare will be before getting in, and ask for a receipt (*paragon*); carefully look over restaurant bills; be extremely wary of handing your passport to anyone who accosts you with a demand for ID; and never exchange money on the street.

Telephones

The country code for the Czech Republic is 420. When dialing a number in the Czech Republic from abroad, drop the initial zero from the regional area code. Prefixes 0601 to 0606 denote mobile phones; when dialing these numbers, no regional area code is needed.

INTERNATIONAL CALLS

To Canada, dial CanadaDirect. To the United Kingdom, dial BT Direct. The operator will connect your collect or credit-card call at the carrier's standard rates. In Prague, many phone booths allow direct international dialing. With the prepaid X Card (300 Kč–1,000 Kč), rates to the U.S. are roughly 22 Kč per minute; a call to the U.K. costs about 14 Kč per minute. If you can't find a booth, the telephone office of the main post office (*see* Mail & Shipping, *above*), open 24 hours, is the best place to try. Once inside, follow signs for TELEGRAF/TELEFAX. The international dialing code is 00. For calls to the United States, Canada, or the United Kingdom, dial the international operator. For inquiries, dial international directory assistance. Otherwise, ask the receptionist at any hotel to put a call through for you, though beware: the more expensive the hotel, the more expensive the call will be.

➤ **Phone Numbers for International Calls: BT Direct** (tel. 00/
4200–4401). **CanadaDirect** (tel. 00/4200–0151). **International
directory assistance** (tel. 1181). **International operator** (tel.
133004).

LOCAL CALLS

Coin-operated pay phones are hard to find. Most newer public
phones operate only with a special telephone card, available
from post offices and newsstands in denominations of 150 Kč
and up. A short call within Prague costs 4 Kč from a coin-
operated phone or the equivalent of 3 Kč (1 unit) from a card-
operated phone. The dial tone is a series of alternating short and
long buzzes.

LONG-DISTANCE SERVICES

AT&T, MCI, and Sprint access codes make calling long distance
relatively convenient, but you may find the local access number
blocked in many hotel rooms. First ask the hotel operator to
connect you. If the hotel operator balks, ask for an international
operator, or dial the international operator yourself. One way to
improve your odds of getting connected to your long-distance
carrier is to travel with more than one company's calling card (a
hotel may block Sprint, for example, but not MCI). If all else fails,
call from a pay phone.

➤ **Access Codes: AT&T Direct** (tel. 00/4200–0101). **MCI
WorldPhone** (tel. 00/4200–0112). **Sprint International Access**
(tel. 00/4208–7187).

Time

The Czech Republic is on Central European Time (CET), one
hour ahead of Greenwich Mean Time and six hours ahead of the
eastern time zone of the United States.

Tipping

Service is usually not included in restaurant bills. **Round the bill
up to the next multiple of 10** (if the bill comes to 83 Kč, for

example, give the waiter 90 Kč); 10% is considered appropriate in all but the most expensive places. Tip porters who bring bags to your rooms 40 Kč total. For room service, a 20 Kč tip is enough. In taxis, round the bill up by 10%. Give tour guides and helpful concierges between 50 Kč and 100 Kč for services rendered.

Train Travel

WITHIN THE CZECH REPUBLIC

The state-run rail system is called České dráhy. On longer runs, it's not really worth taking anything less than an express (*rychlík*) train, marked in red on the timetable. Tickets are still very inexpensive: a second-class ticket from Prague to Brno costs 150 Kč in 2000. First class is considerably more spacious and comfortable and well worth the cost (50% more than a standard ticket). A 60 Kč –85 Kč supplement is charged for the excellent international expresses, EuroCity (EC) and InterCity (IC), and for domestic SuperCity (SC) schedules. A 20 Kč supplement applies to reserved seats on domestic journeys. If you haven't bought a ticket in advance at the station (mandatory for seat reservations), you can buy one aboard the train from the conductor. On timetables, departures (*odjezd*) appear on a yellow background; arrivals (*příjezd*) are on white. It is possible to book sleepers (*lùžkový*) or the less-roomy couchettes (*lehátkový*) on most overnight trains.

Prague is the main gateway to western Bohemia. Major trains from Nuremberg stop at Cheb and usually at Mariánské Lázně; Munich trains cross the border at Česká Kubice. All long-distance trains in the region stop at Plzeň. It is also an easy drive across the border from Bavaria on the E48 to Cheb and from there to any of the spas. Good, if slow, train service links all the major towns west of Prague. The best stretches are from Františkovy Lázně to Plzeň and from Plzeň to Prague. The Prague–Karlovy Vary run takes far longer than it should—more than three hours by the shortest route.

➤ TRAIN INFORMATION: **České dráhy** (ČD; tel. 02/2422–4200 for information, idos.datis.cdrail.cz).

INTERNATIONAL TRAIN TRAVEL

You can take a direct train from Paris via Frankfurt to Prague (daily) or from Berlin via Dresden to Prague (five times a day). Vienna is another good starting point for Prague. There are three trains a day from Vienna's Südbahnhof (South Station) to Prague (five hours). There are no direct trains from London to Prague.

International trains arrive at and depart from either of two stations: The main station, Hlavní nádraží, is about 500 yards east of Wenceslas Square on Opletalova or Washingtonova street. Then there's the suburban Nádraží Holešovice, about 2 km [1 mi] north of the city center. This is an unending source of confusion—always make certain you know which station your train is using. Note also that trains arriving from the west usually stop at Smíchov station, on the west bank of the Vltava, before continuing to the main station. Prague's other central train station, Masarykovo nádraží, serves mostly local trains but has an international ticket window that is often much less crowded than those at the main station. For train times, consult timetables in a station or get in line at the information office upstairs at the main station (for domestic trains; open daily 3 AM–11:45 PM) or downstairs near the exits under the ČD Centrum sign (open daily 6 AM–7:30 PM). The main Čedok office (☞ Visitor Information, *below*) also provides train information and issues tickets.

BETWEEN THE TRAIN
STATION AND THE CITY CENTER

Wenceslas Square is a convenient five-minute walk from the main station (best not undertaken late at night), or you can take the subway (Line C) one stop in the Háje direction to Muzeum. A taxi ride from the main station to the center should cost about 100 Kč, but the station cabbies are known for overcharging. To reach the city center from Nádraží Holešovice, take the metro (Line C) four stops to Muzeum; a taxi ride should cost roughly 200 Kč–250 Kč.

➤ TRAIN STATIONS: **Hlavní nádraží** (Wilsonova ulice). **Masarykovo nádraží** (Hybernská 13; **information office** tel. 02/2422–4200).

RAIL PASSES

Most rail passes, such as the Czech Flexipass, will wind up costing more than what you'd spend buying tickets on the spot, particularly if you intend to travel mainly in the Czech Republic, since international tickets normally are more expensive. The Eurail pass and the Eurail Youthpass are not valid for travel within the Czech Republic. The InterRail pass and the EuroDomino discounted round-trip international ticket are available only to European citizens, or in some cases to people who have been in Europe for six months or longer.

You can use the European East Pass on the national rail networks of the Czech Republic as well as Austria, Hungary, Poland, and Slovakia. The pass covers five days of unlimited first-class travel within a one-month period for $199. Additional travel days may be purchased. You can also combine the East Pass with a national rail pass. A pass for the Czech Republic costs $69 for five days of train travel within a 15-day period—far more than you'd spend on individual tickets.

➤ INFORMATION AND PASSES: **Rail Europe** (500 Mamaroneck Ave., Harrison, NY 10528, tel. 914/682–5172 or 800/438–7245, fax 800/432–1329; 2087 Dundas E, Suite 106, Mississauga, Ontario L4X 1M2, tel. 800/361–7245, fax 905/602–4198). **DER Travel Services** (9501 W. Devon Ave., Rosemont, IL 60018, tel. 800/782–2424, fax 800/282–7474 for information; 800/860–9944 for brochures). **CIT Tours Corp** (15 West 44th Street, 10th Floor, New York, NY 10036, tel. 212/730–2400; 800/248–7245 in the U.S.; 800/387–0711 or 800/361–7799 in Canada).

Travel Agencies

Prague's American Express provides full travel services in addition to changing money and selling traveler's checks. Local Czech travel agencies offer extensive information on regional activities and tours, and larger agencies can supply you with hotel and travel information and book air and rail tickets. Agencies with branches nationwide include Čedok (the former state-owned tourist bureau), Sportturist Special, and Fischer. For bus tickets to just about anywhere in Europe, try Bohemia Tours or Čedok's main office.

➤ LOCAL AGENCIES: **American Express** (Václavské nám. 56, tel. 02/2421–9992, or Mostecká 12, tel. 02/5731–3636, or Vřídelní 51, Karlovy Vary, tel. 017/323–0368). **Bohemia Tour** (Zlatnická 7, tel. 02/231–3925). **Thomas Cook** (Národní třída 28, tel. 02/2110–5276).

Visitor Information

The official provider of tourist information, the Czech Tourist Authority, has offices in the United States, Canada, Great Britain, other countries of Europe, and Japan, as well as Prague. They stock maps and brochures on tourism outside Prague and dispense advice but do not book tickets or accommodations.

There are four central offices of the municipal Prague Information Service (PIS). PIS locates lodging, offers city maps and general tourist information, sells tickets to cultural events, and arranges group and individual tours.

Čedok, the ubiquitous travel agency, provides general tourist information and city maps. Čedok will also exchange money, book accommodations, arrange guided tours, and book passage on airlines, buses, and trains. You can pay for Čedok services, including booking rail tickets, with any major credit card. Note limited weekend hours. The main office is open weekdays 8:30–6 and Saturday 9–1. The Czech Tourist Authority on Old Town Square can provide information on tourism outside Prague but does not sell tickets or book accommodations.

To find out what's on and to get the latest tips for shopping, dining, and entertainment, consult Prague's weekly English-language newspaper, the *Prague Post*. It prints comprehensive entertainment listings and can be bought at most downtown newsstands as well as in major North American and European cities. The monthly *Culture in Prague*, available at newsstands and tourist offices for 40 Kč, provides a good overview of major cultural events.

➤ **Czech Tourist Authority:** Staroměstské nám. 6, tel. 02/2481–0411, www.visitczech.cz (in the U.S.: 1109–1111 Madison Ave., New York, NY 10028, tel. 212/288–0830, fax 212/288–0971, www.czechcenter.com; in Canada: Czech Airlines office, Simpson Tower, 401 Bay St., Suite 1510, Toronto, Ontario M5H 2YA, tel. 416/363–3174, fax 416/363–0239; in the U.K.: 95 Great Portland St., London W1N 5RA, tel. 0171/291–9925, fax 0171/436–8300).

➤ **Prague Information Service: Old Town Hall branch** (Staroměstská radnice [Old Town Hall], tel. 02/2448–2018) is open weekdays 9 to 6 and weekends 9 to 5. **Na Příkopě office** (Na Příkopě 20, tel. 02/264–020) is open weekdays 9 to 6 and Saturday 9 to 3. **Hlavní nádraží branch** (Hlavní nádraží, lower hall, tel. 02/2423–9258) is open from April to October, weekdays 9 to 7 and weekends 9 to 4, and from November to March, weekdays 9 to 6 and Saturday 9 to 3. **Charles Bridge tower office** (Malostranská mostecká věž, tel. 02/536–010), in the tower on the Lesser Quarter end of Charles Bridge, is open April through October only.

➤ **Other Local Agencies:** Čedok (Main office: Na Příkopě 18, tel. 02/2419–7111, fax 02/232–1656). **Czech Tourist Authority** (Staroměstské nám. 6, tel./fax 02/2481–0411).

➤ **In Western Bohemia: Cheb** (Nám. Krále Jiřího z Poděbrad 33, tel. 0166/434–385 or 422–705). **Františkovy Lázně** (Tři Lilie Travel Agency, Národní 3, tel. 0166/542–430). **Karlovy Vary** (Kur-Info,

Vřídelní kolonáda [Vřídlo Colonnade], tel. 017/322–4097, or Nám. Dr. M. Horákové 18 [near the bus station], tel. 017/322–2833). **Mariánské Lázně** (Cultural and Information Center, Hlavní 47, tel. 0165/625–892 or 0165/622–474). **Plzeň** (Nám. Republiky 41, tel. 019/703–2750).

Web Sites

Do check out the World Wide Web when you're planning. You'll find everything from current weather forecasts to virtual tours of famous cities. Fodor's Web site, www.fodors.com, is a great place to start your on-line travels.

When to Go

Prague is beautiful year-round, but avoid midsummer (especially July and August) and the Christmas and Easter holidays, when the city is choked with visitors.

CLIMATE
The following are the average daily maximum and minimum temperatures for Prague.

Jan.	36F	2C	May	66F	19C	Sept.	68F	20C
	25	- 4		46	8		50	10
Feb.	37F	3C	June	72F	22C	Oct.	55F	13C
	27	- 3		52	11		41	5
Mar.	46F	8C	July	75F	24C	Nov.	46F	8C
	32	0		55	13		36	2
Apr.	58F	14C	Aug.	73F	23C	Dec.	37F	3C
	39	4		55	13		28	- 2

➤ FORECASTS: **Weather Channel Connection** (tel. 900/932–8437), 95¢ per minute from a Touch-Tone phone.

176

INDEX

178

FODOR'S POCKET PRAGUE

EDITORS: Bonnie Bills, Hannah Borgeson, Matt Lombardi, Julie Tomasz

EDITORIAL CONTRIBUTORS: Mark Baker, Ky Krauthamer, Martha Lagace

EDITORIAL PRODUCTION: Stacey Kulig

MAPS: David Lindroth, *cartographer;* Bob Blake and Rebecca Baer, *map editors*

DESIGN: Fabrizio La Rocca, *creative director;* Tigist Getachew, *art director;* Melanie Marin, *photo editor*

PRODUCTION/MANUFACTURING: Yexenia M. Markland

COVER PHOTOGRAPH: Barbara Benner/Index Stock

COPYRIGHT

Fourth Edition

ISBN 0-679-00732-6

ISSN 1094-4028

IMPORTANT TIP

Although all prices, opening times, and other details in this book are based on information supplied to us at press time, changes occur all the time in the travel world, and Fodor's cannot accept responsibility for facts that become outdated or for inadvertent errors or omissions. So **always confirm information when it matters,** especially if you're making a detour to visit a specific place.

SPECIAL SALES

PRINTED IN THE UNITED STATES OF AMERICA

10 9 8 7 6 5 4 3 2 1